ART + DATA

CREATED BY DECISIVE DATA

TABLE OF CONTENTS

Aa

WHY DID YOU PICK UP THIS BOOK?

Maybe you're an *executive* who wants quick insights into your organization. You're busy. We get that. You'll probably only skim this book in 20 minutes. But we hope you're compelled by its intuitive visual analytics and the chance to track progress and increase your company's impact. How about getting a box of these books to hand out to your data analytics teams across the company?

Maybe you're a *team lead* who relies on data to fulfill your commitments to your organization. Do you need engaging analytics for your technology group? Sales operations? Finance or marketing program? We're betting yes. Then you'll probably settle in and spend a few hours reading this book and relating to the dashboard examples that best match your department. How about getting 10 or more copies for the other people in your team?

Or maybe you're an *analytics expert*. You geek out on software like Tableau and digging deep into the realm of data visualization. We do too! You'll likely spend days on this book pouring over all the incredible practices and concepts embedded in it. We hope so anyway. Our intent is to highlight best practices for dashboard design and empower you to further explore all those data points we know you're obsessed with. We got your back on this.

No matter who you are, we're sure you'll agree that successful organizations don't just tell data stories—they use excellent design to do so. They find harmony between data and art. We've done just that by creating our *5 Elements of Dashboard Design*: **Integrity**, **Flow**, **Color**, **Typeface** and **Charm**. With these powerful standards, we consistently help people use data to realize better outcomes.

So be inspired. Partner with us. And take from this collection of 20 custom dashboards what you will. Then don't be shy. Blog about it. Recommend it to friends. Put it on the office coffee table. Whatever you do, know that we are one of you!

Luke Hartsock, Decisive Data CEO

Aa ✳

5 ELEMENTS
OF DASHBOARD DESIGN

We love uncovering new data stories with clients and finding solutions to their data quandaries. When we partner with new clients, we get an opportunity to help them visualize data in new ways. While unique data sets require an innovative approach to data visualization, we find that applying a consistent, specific methodology towards design helps us develop the highest quality work.

All the dashboards in this book exemplify our method, which leverages our *5 Elements of Dashboard Design*: **Integrity, Flow, Color, Typeface** and **Charm.** They vary in importance as a dashboard takes shape, but all are critical in assuring that a data story is told in a compelling, accurate and attractive way. We want our final dashboards to stand out.

As you approach data visualization within your organization, we hope you'll find our methodology accessible and exciting. Use this book and the following dashboard examples to learn the *5 Elements* and consider how they might apply in your industry. Imagine the possibilities for beautifully displaying your data story!

INTEGRITY

If visualization is a car, data integrity is its engine.

No matter how beautiful the body, a car's performance is only as good as the engine it carries. The same is true in dashboard development. Developing a fair data analysis precedes dashboard design. Telling a data story with integrity is just as important, if not more important, than how it is presented. Because any data set can be misconstrued, decontextualized or misused, it's imperative that dashboard designers use a variety of metrics and appropriate aggregations when drawing data-driven conclusions for analysts.

Consider a baseball Hall of Famer who had a career batting average of .284, which indicates extraordinary athletic talent. Essentially, he hit the ball more than a quarter of the time throughout his years in the Major Leagues. On the other hand, Tommy Wunhit, who hit a grand slam on his first and only visit to the plate, earned a "career average" of 1.000. Comparing only these two batting averages suggests that our Hall of Famer was the lesser player. But we know that's not the case—Hall of Famers earn that title by dominating the sport for years.

To prove that our Hall of Famer is the better player, we must approach this data set with analytical integrity, which looks at multiple metrics, such as total years played, total home runs hit, and total number of visits to the plate. We might also evaluate these metrics for additional professional baseball players to gain insight into how the two players compare to others. The addition of these metrics illuminate a truth that batting average alone overlooks.

Integrity considers all relevant metrics to tell the full data story accurately. Any and all dashboards can achieve analytical integrity by breaking down complex data sets. This is best accomplished by identifying key metrics, aggregating them correctly, and comparing them in meaningful ways. Doing so helps users make and understand their data-driven decisions.

FLOW

If visualization is a house, flow is its floorplan.

Individual rooms within a house may be well decorated and furnished, but a home that lacks a logical floor plan does not facilitate day-to-day convenience. It simply doesn't flow well. Now imagine a dashboard comprised of informative visuals but lacking any clues that guide the user through the information. Without good flow that helps direct the dashboard user, even intuitive visualizations can be confusing. Flow uses visual clues, creates momentum and establishes clear paths for data discovery.

When it comes to engaging users, the location of visual clues matters. Users should be able to easily identify dashboard functionality and know where to start and how to move through a dashboard. These clues often highlight elements like filters and buttons that allow users to slice the data and explore a more granular analysis. When properly encouraged and guided through the data story, users will want to continue investigating detailed information. If users don't immediately identify how to interact with the dashboard, they are less likely to engage and understand how the details interrelate.

Flow creates visual momentum within a dashboard. Momentum leads users from one visualization to the next as they explore more granular data and piece together the data story. Visual elements within a dashboard should make a unique and meaningful contribution to the overarching narrative. In other words, flow is guaranteed when the visualizations fit logically within the framework of the data story.

Each visualization should also inspire users to continue exploring the data thus establishing momentum and keeping users engaged. This momentum can move in a variety of directions, but it always establishes consistent engagement paths for users. Dashboards that have exceptional flow resonate with users because they offer relevant information in a meaningful sequence.

COLOR

If visualization is a stage, color is a spotlight.

Just as a spotlight draws an audience to what's relevant on stage, color helps dashboard users focus on the most important data. A lack of color can blur the data story and cause confusion, much like how a dark stage can confuse an audience. On the contrary, too much color can overwhelm and distract from the dashboard's critical features. Color should be deliberate, consistent and meaningful to help users form valuable conclusions.

Hue, shade and tint all come into play when picking the perfect palette. For example, distinctive colors can be used to call action and highlight key metrics, while neutral colors might be reserved for contextual data. However, it's not enough to simply use certain complementary colors in dashboard design. There are other considerations like contrast/brightness, customization and color restraint to maximize the use of color.

Color has an instantaneous effect on the human brain, so first impressions are crucial. If the contrast and/or brightness of a color palette is too severe, users may disengage without realizing why. Default color choices might be quick and convenient, but they can also be overwhelmingly bright and generic. A custom color palette demonstrates that the designer has invested time to create a higher-end dashboard with more attention to the nuances of detail. Colors can be strategically selected and fine-tuned to fit the specific needs and theme of each dashboard thus giving a customized appearance.

When it comes to color, less is more. Many excellent dashboards use only one color or a gradient of just one color, which can lend itself to an elegant monochrome effect. Conversely, a prominent color can spotlight specific data while gray can be used for less important data. Traffic lights are a great example. They have three colors, but the three are never lit up at the same time. If they were, drivers wouldn't know what to do. The same is true for a dashboard. One color emphasizing what's important is more effective than everything being emphasized equally.

Aa

TYPEFACE

If visualization is a photo, typeface is a filter.

Instagram became wildly popular as people began posting real-time photos draped in nostalgic filters. Users discovered the power of changing filters to create a different look and feel to identical photographs. Much like these filters, typeface can evoke emotion such as nostalgia, excitement or urgency. A strategic use of typeface, which considers font style and size as well as modifications like boldface, italics and spacing, greatly influences how text is communicated. Typeface doesn't change the content, but it does impact the message and tone.

Take, for example, well-known font families like Helvetica and Times. They're classics and widely used for large blocks of text. Arial and Verdana are also universal and functional. Others, like Grenadier and Riesling are more nostalgic. And the clean lines of Museo have a contemporary feel.

Also consider what's appropriate. Titles and headers, for instance, can be decorative but should always capture the desired tone. Invitations are a good example. They use typeface to establish whether an event is more formal or casual; grand or intimate. Likewise, a dashboard's typeface sets expectations for users.

Font size and weight are other effective ways to communicate information because they help create organizational hierarchy. Generally, dashboard titles appear larger than visualization headers, which appear larger than text for labels, axes and auxiliary data. This variance in text size or emphasis with bold or italics, for example, provides visual clues to users about data granularity and dashboard organization.

No matter the choices, careful attention to style, size and weight will ensure that the typeface will both drive a dashboard's message and help visually organize information.

C H A R M

If visualization is a book, charm is its cover.

You've heard it said, "Don't judge a book by its cover." This is a popular phrase because people, by nature, often make snap judgments. Similar to a book's cover, a dashboard's charm is usually the first thing a user notices. For this reason, it's imperative that charm not only reinforces a dashboard's overall narrative but also instantly attracts and engages users. Admittedly charm is a subjective element. But there are ways to implement charm and invoke a positive response. Simple icons, relevant branding and appropriate images are effective in making dashboards memorable.

Using customized images that are consistent with a dashboard's color and general design is a great way to add charm. They provide visual variance and can sometimes inspire color palettes and aesthetic themes. They should also be relevant and contribute in some way to the subject matter. Using icons, especially within a header or title, is another way to incorporate charm. They can be decorative, reinforce themes, and even provide visual communication.

Reinforcing a company's or organization's brand can also lend charm to a dashboard. Adding a company logo is a simple yet effective way to engage users while also enforcing brand identity. Logos keep charm relevant. As visual analytics gain popularity among organizations across industries, it's important that even internal tools use elements that align an analytics dashboard with an organization's brand.

Adding charm to a dashboard may not always be necessary, but even the simplest detail can stick with users and make the analytics more memorable. So whether using graphic images, icons, logos or all of the above, they'll go a long way towards engaging users and cementing a visual understanding of the data story.

13

20 DASHBOARDS

Simply introducing the *5 Elements of Dashboard Design* is not sufficient to empower you to produce high-quality visualizations. We must also demonstrate in detail how these *5 Elements* apply to dashboards, especially across a variety of industries. Following are 20 custom dashboards from a wide range of fields and markets. While some examples are more transferrable than others, they all exemplify the methodology we apply to excellent visual analytics. We hope you find examples that speak to your industry and personal interests.

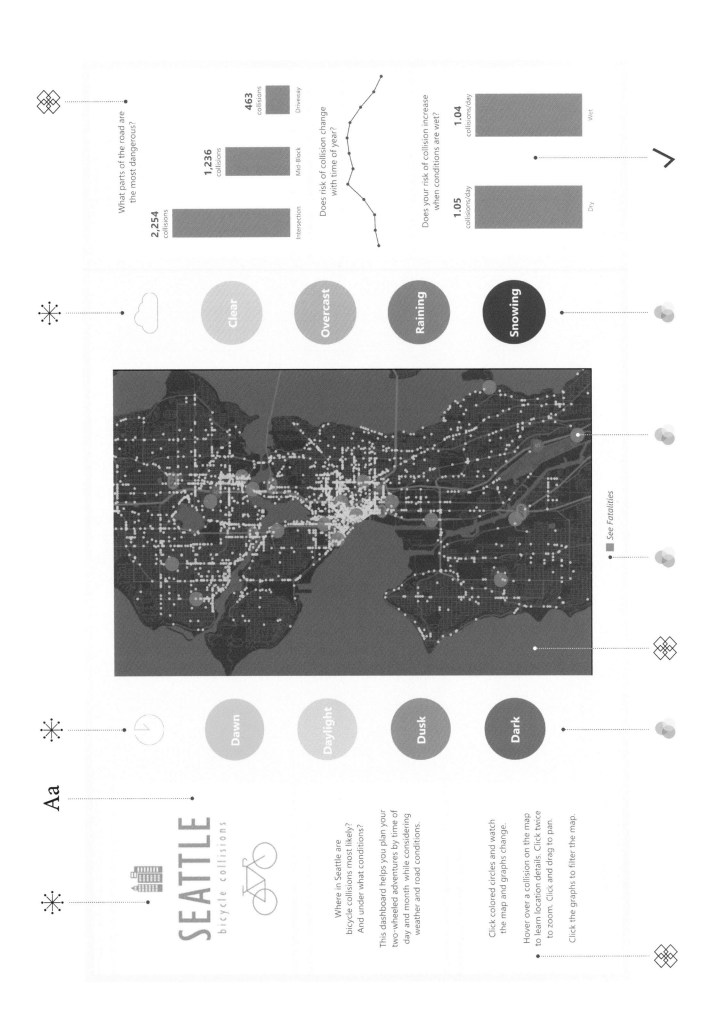

SEATTLE
bicycle collisions

Where in Seattle are bicycle collisions most likely? And under what conditions?

This dashboard helps you plan your two-wheeled adventures by time of day and month while considering weather and road conditions.

Click colored circles and watch the map and graphs change.

Hover over a collision on the map to learn location details. Click twice to zoom. Click and drag to pan.

Click the graphs to filter the map.

Clear
Overcast
Raining
Snowing

Dawn
Daylight
Dusk
Dark

See Fatalities

What parts of the road are the most dangerous?

2,254 collisions — Intersection
1,236 collisions — Mid-Block
463 collisions — Driveway

Does risk of collision change with time of year?

Does your risk of collision increase when conditions are wet?

1.05 collisions/day — Dry
1.04 collisions/day — Wet

SEATTLE BICYCLE COLLISIONS

Data and information for the public's use is increasingly available through public institutions. Downloading this data may be easy, but engaging with it, usually in a spreadsheet format, is not. Sadly, the vast amount of information for public consumption is wasted if not effectively communicated. However, strong visualizations of public-facing data sets allow people to better engage with the information.

This dashboard about Seattle's bicycle collision rates (based on a seattle.gov data set) is one such example. Cycling is an increasingly popular means of urban transportation. As Seattle's population increases, so do the risks associated with cycling in the city.

What does this dashboard teach users? Bicycle collisions happen frequently and throughout the city. Cyclists traveling through higher density areas of Seattle face higher risk of collision. Collisions occur in all sorts of road configurations but most likely at intersections. And, although rare, bicycle collisions are sometimes fatal.

Some of these conclusions may seem obvious, but the dashboard also debunks common misconceptions. Fair skies and dry weather, for instance, don't necessarily ensure a safer ride. Collisions occur in all sorts of weather and daylight. As the lower right visualization illustrates, the likelihood of a collision is nearly the same whether roads are wet or dry.

Through data storytelling, the City of Seattle has a strong means of educating the community around bicycle safety. People can see and better understand the risks involved in urban cycling and make important decisions about those risks.

Analytical **integrity** is maintained by appropriately comparing the data between dry conditions and wet. If more information exists for dry conditions, the data could suggest that dry conditions are more dangerous based on collision volume alone. To avoid misinforming and to fairly compare dry and wet conditions, collisions per day relative to rider volume must also be considered.

The left column establishes **flow** by featuring the title and background information and introducing the interactive colored filters. Momentum then moves into the map from both the left and right filter buttons. Flow continues to the right column where users can explore granular data based on their color selections.

Color is used to highlight the interactive filters. Time of day is reinforced visually with appropriate colors and hues. Likewise, increased weather severity visually increases with darker shades of blue. Shades of gray are used throughout the rest of this dashboard, allowing the colored filters to draw users into the central functionality.

Avi Sans, a large, decorative **typeface**, is used in the title. It's clean and contemporary for a largely young, urban Seattle population. Segoe UI is used elsewhere, making it easy for users to read smaller text on this dashboard.

This dashboard implements **charm** with two custom images: a small city skyline above the title and a bicycle image beneath. Both are gray to match the aesthetic of the dashboard layout and are logical visual representations of the topic. The clock and cloud outline images also add a level of charm.

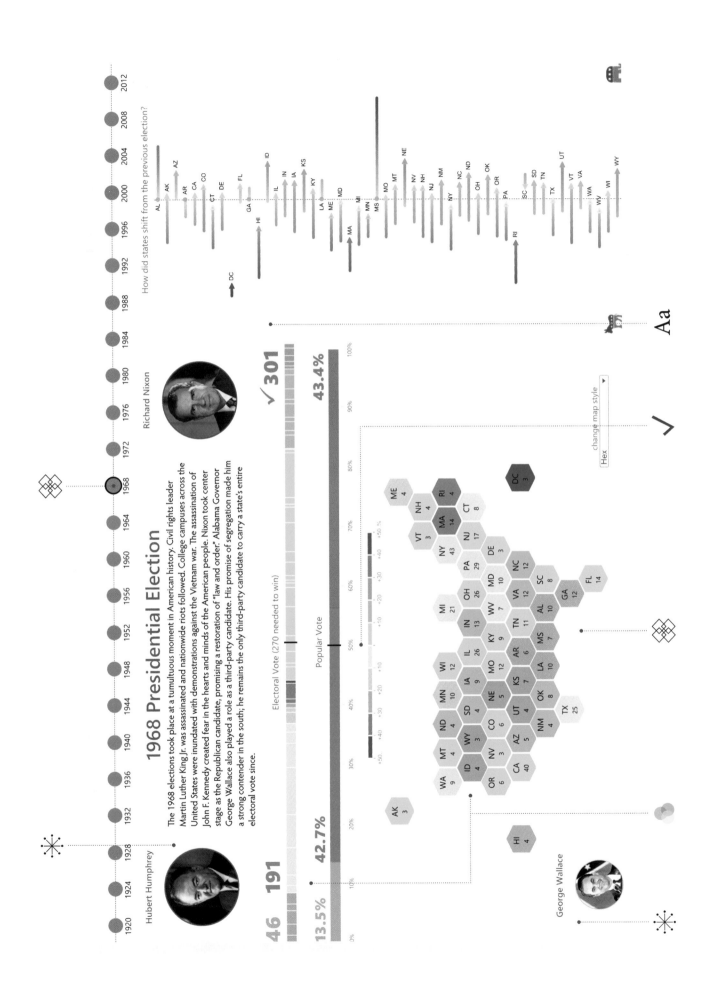

1968 Presidential Election

Hubert Humphrey

Richard Nixon

The 1968 elections took place at a tumultuous moment in American history. Civil rights leader Martin Luther King Jr. was assassinated and nationwide riots followed. College campuses across the United States were inundated with demonstrations against the Vietnam war. The assassination of John F. Kennedy created fear in the hearts and minds of the American people. Nixon took center stage as the Republican candidate, promising a restoration of "law and order." Alabama Governor George Wallace also played a role as a third-party candidate. His promise of segregation made him a strong contender in the south; he remains the only third-party candidate to carry a state's entire electoral vote since.

How did states shift from the previous election?

1920 1924 1928 1932 1936 1940 1944 1948 1952 1956 1960 1964 1968 1972 1976 1980 1984 1988 1992 1996 2000 2004 2008 2012

Electoral Vote (270 needed to win)

46   191   √ 301

Popular Vote

13.5%   42.7%   43.4%

0%   10%   20%   30%   40%   50%   60%   70%   80%   90%   100%

+50 +40 +30 +20 +10   +10 +20 +30 +40 +50 %

George Wallace

change map style

Hex

Aa

AK 3

HI 4

WA 9   ID 4   MT 4   ND 4   MN 10   WI 12   MI 21   ME 4
OR 6   NV 3   WY 3   SD 4   IA 9   IL 26   IN 13   OH 26   PA 29   NY 43   VT 3   NH 4   MA 14   RI 4
CA 40   AZ 5   CO 6   NE 5   MO 12   KY 9   WV 7   VA 12   MD 10   NJ 17   CT 8
         UT 4   KS 7   AR 6   TN 11   NC 12   DE 3
NM 4   OK 8   LA 10   MS 7   AL 10   SC 8
TX 25   GA 12   FL 14

DC 3

US PRESIDENTIAL ELECTIONS

As journalism continues to occupy space online, content receives more and more views. Visual aids must be simultaneously accurate and eye-catching. In a world of social media, smart phones, and constant internet access, consistently capturing the public's attention takes an act of creative genius. Media sources must also dispense reliable and accurate information to give the public important and relevant topics.

With an election cycle every four years, Americans pay more attention to presidential candidates and the issues that will determine who wins. Media outlets respond to increased interest in this topic. As candidates take center stage, blogs, newspapers and magazines dive into relevant data that feeds the public's interest on the subject.

This dashboard relays a tremendous amount of historical data about presidential elections in the United States. The unique, interactive year filter along the top gives users a general idea of how party popularity has fluctuated over time. When a year is selected, users see the dashboard change to reflect state-level details about that election.

Although this dashboard speaks specifically to American politics, it demonstrates what it takes to capture a user's attention for long periods of time. The volume of data presented, along with the complexity and depth of the visualizations, inspires users to engage and explore over and over again.

To tell US political stories with **integrity,** you must capture the nuance of party support. Voters should not be allocated into one of two buckets. More categories are needed to evaluate not only what party took the majority but also by how much. Integrating the independent party impacts how intensely left or right a state leans. As a result, this dashboard illustrates a wide spectrum of blues and reds.

The time filter at the top of this dashboard establishes **flow** by guiding users through presidential election data between 1920 through 2012. This filter gives additional information by displaying the winning party, giving users a high-level summary of political shifts.

This dashboard uses conventional political **colors**—blue and red—to represent the two primary American political parties. In contrast, yellow appears on election cycles that had significant third-party support. These conventional colors are reinforced to indicate the winning party for past elections and with an appropriate frame around a candidate's photo. States are colored based on their Electoral Vote majority on the map and political shift chart.

Aa This dashboard uses the Segoe **typeface,** which aligns well with many online publications. It's familiar, easy to read, and allows users to focus on content and data trends. Larger, bold text highlights electoral results and draws users to the most important values in this data story.

Candidate photos help bring **charm** to this dashboard. Because US presidential elections include well-known world leaders in history, users are instantly drawn into the visuals by faces they recognize. The hex map is also a special feature of this dashboard and intrigues users with an unconventional, modern map of the United States.

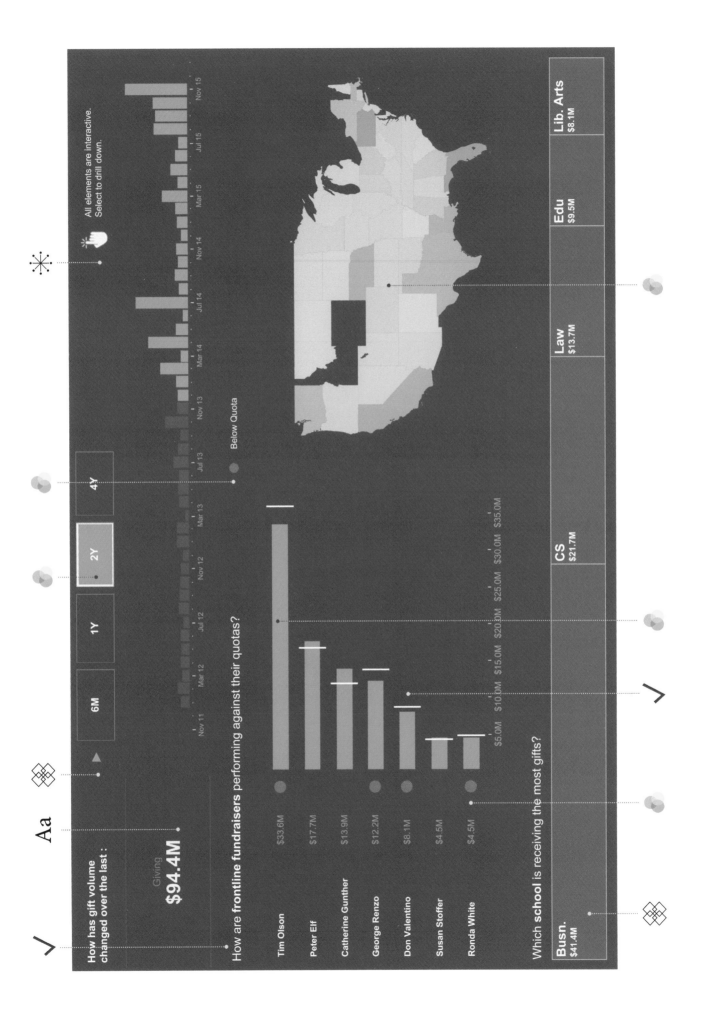

How has gift volume changed over the last :

Giving
$94.4M

6M   1Y   2Y   4Y

All elements are interactive.
Select to drill down.

How are frontline fundraisers performing against their quotas?

Tim Olson $33.6M
Peter Elf $17.7M
Catherine Gunther $13.9M
George Renzo $12.2M
Don Valentino $8.1M
Susan Stoffer $4.5M
Ronda White $4.5M

$5.0M $10.1M $15.0M $20.0M $25.0M $30.0M $35.0M

Below Quota

Which **school** is receiving the most gifts?

Busn.
$41.4M

CS
$21.7M

Law
$13.7M

Edu
$9.5M

Lib. Arts
$8.1M

ANNUAL ALUMNI GIVING

Building strong relationships with alumni to increase philanthropic support is central to any academic institution. Organizational leadership must identify the ideal professionals to deepen these relationships. That's a challenge and poses many questions: How many alumni donors should be carried in a portfolio? Where should an organization deploy its fundraising resources geographically? How are frontline fundraisers performing against goals? Fundraising data supports organizational leadership to answer these questions by identifying top performers, establishing goals, tracking success and evaluating overall performance.

This dashboard looks at that data over four years. As we approached this data set, we sliced it by defined periods to see trends over time without getting too granular. This allows users to see dollar volume by month for the entire four-year period as well as a more focused two-year, one-year or six-month view.

The list ranking frontline fundraisers is a powerful component, as it changes when we slice the data by time. For example, Tim Olsen is a top performer across all time periods, but he consistently misses his goals. Conversely, Peter Elf generally achieves his goals for every time period, except when looking at the last six months. The map offers more insight, illustrating how gifts are distributed geographically. It updates with the time period selected and allows users to select a frontline fundraiser to see how individual activities compare across states. Additionally, the lower tree map provides auxiliary information about which schools ultimately receive gifts.

These insights raise meaningful questions for leadership: Does Tim need to be cross-trained with Phil to share best practices? Does Tim's portfolio have too many alumni donors? Is Peter's portfolio robust enough to leverage his fundraising skills? By answering these questions with the aid of this dashboard's powerful visuals, the organization can evaluate its performance and identify high-impact fundraisers.

Establishing a quota for fundraisers is imperative to this data story. Special care must be taken to ensure fundraisers are assigned appropriate quotas, but also that those quotas are easily understood. **Integrity** is implemented by reinforcing quotas in two ways: a reference line compared to actuals and a red indicator to highlight missed quotas.

At the top of this dashboard, a green, right-pointing arrow establishes **flow** by inviting users to select a time period and filter the data. Upon selecting, corresponding months highlight on the bar chart with a fixed, four-year axis. The visualizations below also filter. Downward momentum then takes users to the tree map, which breaks down donations by school.

The muted green with its dark, charcoal background and light text make a sophisticated palette. As green typically represents money, it's a logical choice for this dashboard's prominent **color** and directs users to donation volume throughout. The same green highlights the time period filter, if selected. Red, a strong contrasting color, is used exclusively to indicate donors that fall below quota.

This dashboard also serves as a workplace, so the **typeface** shouldn't distract. It uses Arial because the font is simple, easy to read, and more functional than decorative. A hierarchy of importance is also established with font size. High-level values and titles are largest, while paragraph and label text is small and consistent.

Everything on this dashboard is clickable as indicated by the selection icon at the top right. Visual clues add **charm** and are the simplest and fastest way to tell users that they can engage with all dashboard elements. The map also adds charm. Not only does it illustrate the geographic distribution of donations, its unique design seamlessly integrates into the dashboard's background.

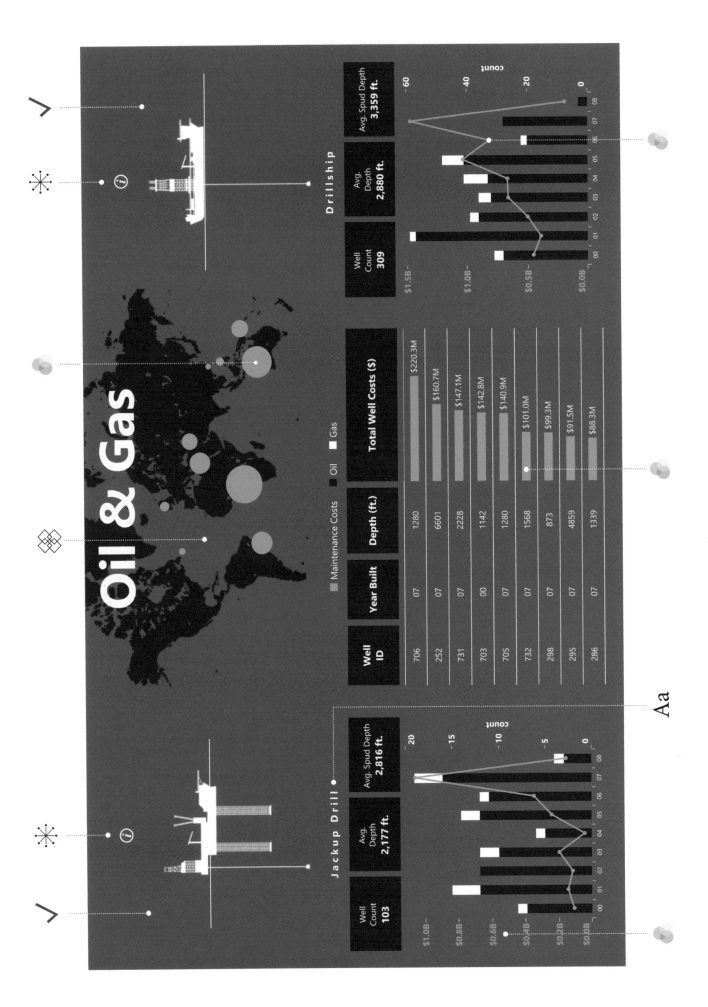

OIL & GAS FACILITY MAINTENANCE

Keeping close watch on maintenance expenditures is important for businesses that rely on specialized facilities or equipment to supply their product. While maintenance costs impact overall revenue short term, they also dictate price point increases and help develop long-term revenue goals. Increasing maintenance costs coupled with unchanged product pricing means profits will dip into the red.

This dashboard tracks data for an oil and gas company that has various types of drills in many locations around the world. It reflects both oil and gas data from individual drills, making granular analysis possible. The world map is a filter that leverages geographic data, allowing users to look at drills in one or many locations. Data is also sliced by drill type to effectively compare the two side by side.

As users select geographic locations, they learn relevant information about these drill types such as the count of wells for that region and type, depth of drill, and spud depth. These measures change dynamically and help users gain insight into key metrics about a well or group of wells including actual costs. Bar charts on the bottom left and right show years in which costs exceeded revenue. More granular information about individual wells is located in the center, helping users identify wells that have high maintenance costs. Having easy access to this well-specific information may ultimately dictate which wells the company continues to maintain.

Companies like this often collect data that measures maintenance costs, but they don't always leverage that data visually to help to answer questions as quickly and easily as possible. Ultimately, every company can benefit from the ability to visually identify where costs exceed profits.

The original data set contained information for three well types, but this dashboard only displays two. The third well type was removed because the associated data was not robust. Assuring that all sheets display data relevant to only the well types shown maintains analytical **integrity**. Neglecting to remove the third well type consistently throughout would result in inaccurate visualizations.

A filter map provides the first step for users and begins the **flow** of this dashboard. Secondly, users are directed down to a list of wells that account for their selection(s) on the map. The third step directs users either right or left, where they view detailed information about different well types.

A blue, black and gray **color** palette strongly invokes the hues of oil and gas. Blue is used exclusively for well maintenance costs in both the map and the lower line charts to draw focus against this dashboard's multiple metrics. This specific color blue both complements and provides contrast to the dark aesthetic.

Aa

Segoe, chosen for its clean, modern aesthetic, is the only **typeface** used in this dashboard. The font size establishes an organization hierarchy, starting with the title, which is significantly larger than the rest of the text. The summary tiles use bold fonts to draw attention and emphasis to those values. Increased letter spacing, or "tracking," is used to differentiate the drill type names from other elements.

Custom icons of each well type visually divide the data and educate users about how the well types differ to help them compare. Small information buttons also help educate users about the well types. Both visual communication methods exemplify **charm.**

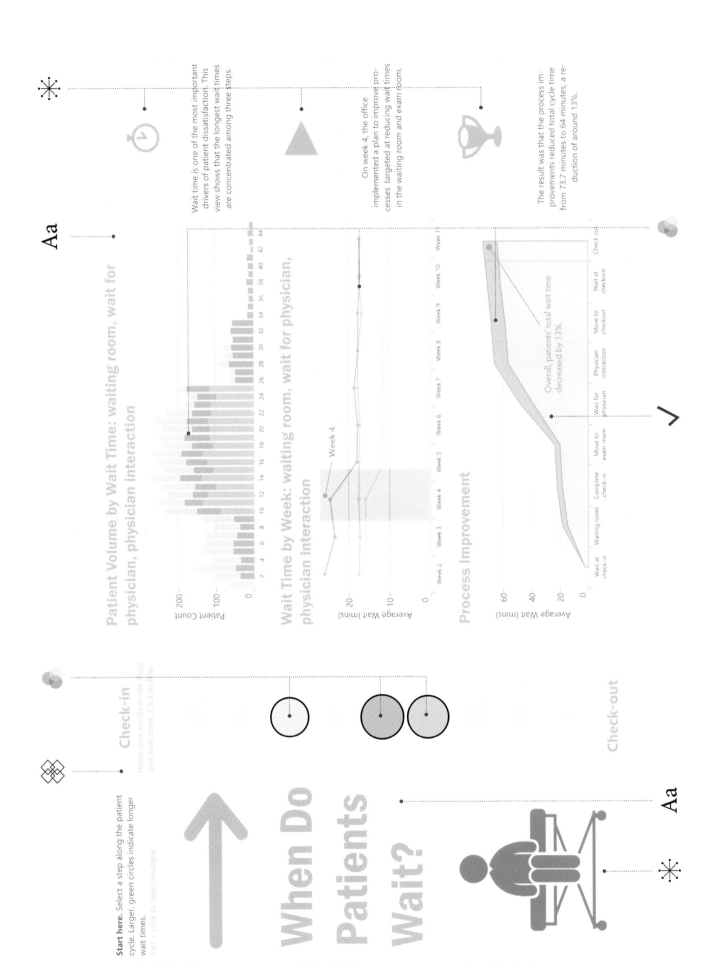

When Do Patients Wait?

Start here. Select a step along the patient cycle. Larger, green circles indicate longer wait times.
Ctrl + click to select multiple

Check-in

Hover over circles to see steps and wait times. Click to filter

Check-out

Patient Volume by Wait Time: waiting room, wait for physician, physician interaction

Patient Count

Wait time is one of the most important drivers of patient dissatisfaction. This view shows that the longest wait times are concentrated among three steps.

Wait Time by Week: waiting room, wait for physician, physician interaction

Average Wait (mins)

Week 4

Week 2 Week 3 Week 4 Week 5 Week 6 Week 7 Week 8 Week 9 Week 10 Week 11

On week 4, the office implemented a plan to improve processes targeted at reducing wait times in the waiting room and exam room.

Process Improvement

Average Wait (mins)

Wait at check-in | Waiting room | Complete check-in | Move to exam room | Wait for physician | Physician interaction | Move to checkout | Wait at checkout | Check out

Overall, patients' total wait time decreased by 13%.

The result was that the process improvements reduced total cycle time from 73.7 minutes to 64 minutes, a reduction of around 13%.

HEALTHCARE LOGISTICS
PATIENT WAIT CYCLE

From taco trucks to dental clinics, many companies depend on customer reviews to make business decisions. A couple of bad comments on Yelp, for example, can seriously damage a company's reputation, so it's important to provide positive customer experiences. Profitability ultimately depends on it. Customer service data can help any organization learn where to improve processes for its customers.

This dashboard considers the patient cycle at a health clinic that monitors patients between check-in and check-out. It explores the amount of time patients wait. Any poor reviews this clinic receives on long wait times is valuable information.

The visualization identifies the three biggest contributors to patient wait time: the waiting room, wait for physician, and physician interaction. While interacting with a physician is likely not the cause of patient dissatisfaction, patients who experience delays in the waiting and exam rooms could become frustrated. More granular information, such as the center top histogram, breaks down how many patients waited for a given amount of time.

Beyond identifying wait-time problems, this dashboard actually illustrates process improvement. In week four of data collection, this clinic implemented an improved system to update patient charts. Strong analytics leverage the data to help this clinic track improvement. Although this dashboard is specific to healthcare, the principles are highly transferable to any client-based field. Data-driven decisions can greatly impact efforts to improve customer satisfaction.

The lower right chart displays an average running total of patient wait times throughout the patient cycle. Running a total aggregation of wait times, and showing an accumulation of time saved, satisfies analytical **integrity**. Users can analyze the wait cycle holistically, rather than for discrete portions of the cycle.

The words "Start here" on the upper left section introduce this dashboard and give instructions. They also establish a top-to-bottom **flow** that is carried throughout the sections. Additionally, the large arrow pushes users from left to right as they explore increasingly detailed information.

Green tones on a white background were chosen as a subtle nod to the sterile environment of a health clinic. Since longer wait times are the most important metric in this dashboard, **color** is used only on portions of the patient cycle that represent the longest wait periods. Gradient colors help differentiate the three different cycle steps that contribute most to longer waits.

Aa

Fonts from the Franklin **typeface** are used to make the title and visualization headers stand out. In contrast, Segoe UI is used for smaller, auxiliary text. While there are many other appropriate typefaces for this dashboard, Franklin and Segoe font families are excellent choices that produce a sharp, modern aesthetic.

Custom images communicate the theme of this dashboard even before users read a single word. The waiting patient icon on the lower left represents the subject, which is reinforced by the clock icon on the upper right. The large arrow on the upper left uniquely kick-starts momentum for users. The trophy highlights the improvements made by the staff. This visual communication exemplifies **charm**.

Decisive Data University

Instructor: Barney, Petra

Course: Advanced 12 Theory

How are my students doing overall?

Student	Grade	
Barnett, James	B+	89.58
Byers, Alex	C+	79.17
Cash, Franklin	A	93.96
Castille, Moira	B+	88.44
Downing, Troy	D	66.04
Foster, Hank	A-	90.94
Hunter, Chelsea	A-	91.56
Jenkins, Dale	F	62.71
Kinner, Cole	B+	88.65
LaMonte, Carla	A-	90.52
Lehmann, Leonard	C	75.73
Niezgoda, Maria	B-	81.56
Martin, Kyle	B	86.15
Montenegro, Angela	B+	88.23
Ortblad, Jessica	A-	91.15
Risdale, Tyler	A	94.06
Theory, Sarah	A	95.94

How are my students doing with assignments?

Legend: Missing | Late | Complete

Students:
Barnett, James; Byers, Alex; Cash, Franklin; Castille, Moira; Downing, Troy; Foster, Hank; Hunter, Chelsea; Jenkins, Dale; Kinner, Cole; LaMonte, Carla; Lehmann, Leonard; Niezgoda, Maria; Martin, Kyle; Montenegro, Angela; Ortblad, Jessica; Risdale, Tyler; Theory, Sarah

What is my course grade distribution?

Student Count axis: 0, 5, 10
Grade categories: A, A-, B, B-, B+, C, C+, D, F

What is the late assignment trend?

Axis: 0, 10, 20
Dates: Jul 15, Aug 15, Sep 15

What is the missing assignment trend?

Axis: 0, 10, 20
Dates: Jul 15, Aug 15, Sep 15

CLASSROOM EVALUATION

Identifying problem areas is vital to any organization's improvement. A classroom is no exception. Generally high-performing students have more opportunities and resources as they progress to higher education. To help students progress, teachers need a strong understanding of whether or not students are meeting expectations.

This dashboard illustrates how data can empower teachers by helping them identify students needing additional support. On the far left, students are ranked by average grade. This shows users how students compare to their peers overall. Although the ranking is helpful, users need a more granular view of student assignments to assess why a student might be struggling.

Assignment-level data helps users understand why students are achieving a given grade. Missing and late assignments are highlighted, so users can see trends, identify struggling students, and develop a plan to give students an opportunity to better meet assignment deadlines. Identifying struggling students and helping them avoid missing assignments is a simple way to help students achieve higher grades and increase their engagement.

Other visualizations look at assignments over time. This provides global insight to student performance and helps users ask important questions: Does this student miss assignments sporadically or regularly? Do missing and late assignments have patterns week over week? Is there a discrete period of time in which a student has missed assignments? Could there be other factors contributing to a student's poor performance?

Performance data informs users and illustrates a student's experience. Without this insight, users may not see important trends that call for intervention that could benefit a student. In this context, data can help teachers build relationships with students that may need more support in achieving their academic goals.

The **integrity** of the line charts that visualize the late and missing assignment trends is strengthened by matching the y-axes to each other and showing the same range of values. This is better than formatting to y-axes with different ranges because users can compare late and missing assignments on the same scale.

This dashboard follows a basic top-to-bottom, left-to-right **flow**. However, the size of the visualizations indicates what's most important thus skewing the flow. For instance, the grid displaying student assignments is very large and focuses users into the core of this data story.

Bright, contrasting **colors** are used strictly for missing and late assignments to put focus on that data. All other items, including assignments completed on time, are gray because this dashboard is designed to help users identify struggling students. Color anywhere else would be distracting and ineffective to the dashboard's objective.

Trebuchet MS is used on this dashboard. This **typeface** is appropriate for workplace dashboards because it provides some variance from standard Helvetic fonts, but isn't so decorative as to distract users from analysis. Headings appear as bigger, white text on a black background to call attention to this dashboard's subject.

The **charm** on this dashboard is simple but effective. The footer contains a copyright icon, giving credit to the author organization. Such details are often overlooked and excluded, but they give dashboards a polished feel as users explore their contents.

Physician Engagement

1 Does it matter how pharmaceutical companies contact physicians about new drugs? Select a campaign type and see how prescription volume correlates with campaign types.

Solicitations Sent:	Unique Drugs Prescribed:	Prescription Count:
27	10	351

2 Select a physician. The bar chart to the right filters to all prescriptions written by that physician.

Prescription Volume by Drug

Physician Name	Brand	
Albert Ng	Accitrope	0 Rx
	Alista	9 Rx
	Erbitol	36 Rx
	Meritux	22 Rx
Jack Han	Affiniox	0 Rx
Jason Vieh	Meritux	24 Rx
Jennifer Martinez	Accitrope	18 Rx
	Erbitol	0 Rx
	Fenofara 3%	10 Rx
Jill Harris	Humadine XR	25 Rx
	Novochol	6 Rx
Marissa Neher	Affiniox	0 Rx
	Juvilex	21 Rx
Mark Mendel	Accitrope	0 Rx
	Affiniox	16 Rx
	Corovera	0 Rx
	Erbitol	12 Rx
	Fenofara 3%	6 Rx
Suzanna Pondel	Erbitol	16 Rx
Tamara Han	Meritux	31 Rx
	Affiniox	11 Rx
Tom Garson	Humadine XR	14 Rx

3 Select a bar. These represent the number of prescriptions each physician has written for each drug. The bar chart below will filter yet again to show the volume of prescriptions for that specific drug and when they were written.

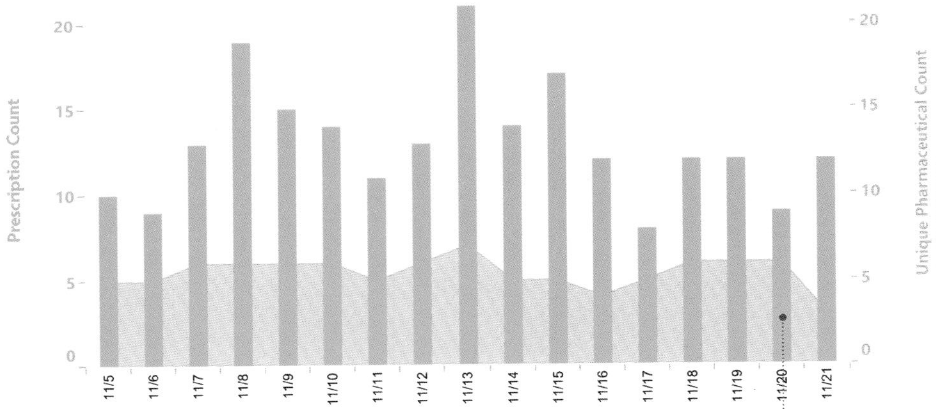

Prescription Count / Unique Pharmaceutical Count — dates: 11/5, 11/6, 11/7, 11/8, 11/9, 11/10, 11/11, 11/12, 11/13, 11/14, 11/15, 11/16, 11/17, 11/18, 11/19, 11/20, 11/21

PHARMACEUTICALS
PHYSICIAN ENGAGEMENT

Marketing data can help answer important questions about customer engagement. This dashboard explores how a pharmaceutical company reaches out to physicians via three campaign types: email, mail and in-person visits. The data includes information about how and when physicians were contacted, how many prescriptions they wrote, and for which drugs.

Users start by selecting a communication method to reveal a list of physicians who receive that type of engagement. That list also includes a measure indicating how many prescriptions the physicians wrote.

Continuing on to select an individual physician, users see in the black summary tiles and lower right graph dynamic information about that physician alone, such as: the number of solicitations a physician received, the total prescriptions they wrote, and the number of unique drugs that are represented in the total prescriptions.

Users learn whether or not an increase in solicitations causes a physician to diversify the drugs they prescribe to patients. They also learn which marketing efforts correlate with an uptick in a physician's prescription diversification. Physicians who like to prescribe new drugs after learning about them will be more receptive to future solicitations.

Pharmaceutical companies can use this information to strategically choose how best to contact physicians. They can also identify physicians who are receptive to prescribing new drugs. Subsequently, any company seeking to optimize its marketing efforts and target high-potential customers can leverage these concepts.

 By including the unique count of unique drugs, the **integrity** of this data story significantly increases. It wouldn't be as useful to pharmaceutical sales to only list a total count of prescriptions written since a physician who prescribes many different drugs is usually more receptive to marketing outreach.

 The **flow** of this dashboard moves generally from left to right but is also very fluid. Momentum is maintained by the user's ability to select visualizations and further filter the information. The large, bold numbers reinforce this key component and uniquely guide users through navigating this dashboard's selection options.

 Color is used sparingly to highlight the prescription volume of unique drugs prescribed by physicians. Orange, in particular, was inspired by the color of pill bottles conventionally used in pharmacies. Using this one color is a deliberate effort to highlight one metric that indicates how likely a physician is to prescribe new drugs.

Aa Franklin and Segoe **typefaces** appear in this dashboard. However, the font sizes vary, most notably with the large numbers that guide users to selection and filter opportunities. Instructions that accompany the oversized numbers are small and italicized. This text differs from data-relevant data, which appears as normal, small text.

 The stethoscope image in the upper left corner is a clear, visual clue that instantly identifies and reinforces this dashboard's subject matter. Likewise, the campaign type filter uses icons to denote outreach methods, which adds to the visual **charm**.

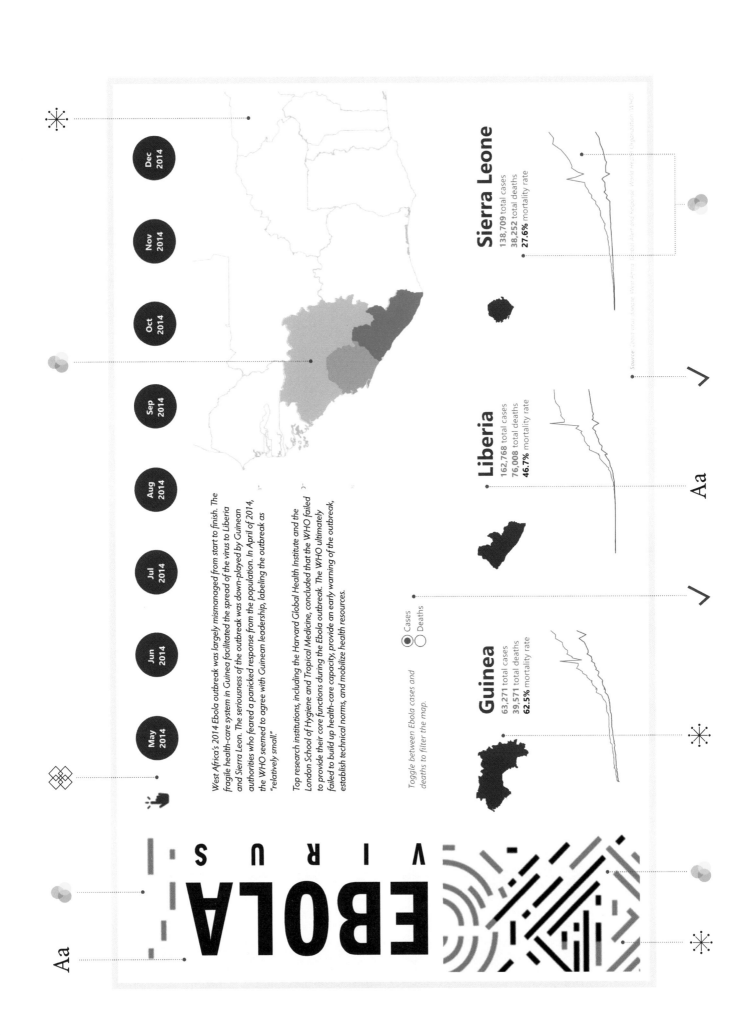

EBOLA VIRUS

May 2014 · Jun 2014 · Jul 2014 · Aug 2014 · Sep 2014 · Oct 2014 · Nov 2014 · Dec 2014

West Africa's 2014 Ebola outbreak was largely mismanaged from start to finish. The fragile health-care system in Guinea facilitated the spread of the virus to Liberia and Sierra Leon. The seriousness of the outbreak was down-played by Guinean authorities who feared a panicked response from the population. In April of 2014, the WHO seemed to agree with Guinean leadership, labeling the outbreak as "relatively small."

Top research institutions, including the Harvard Global Health Institute and the London School of Hygiene and Tropical Medicine, concluded that the WHO failed to provide their core functions during the Ebola outbreak. The WHO ultimately failed to build up health-care capacity, provide an early warning of the outbreak, establish technical norms, and mobilize health resources.

Toggle between Ebola cases and deaths to filter the map.

◉ Cases
○ Deaths

Guinea
63,271 total cases
39,571 total deaths
62.5% mortality rate

Liberia
162,768 total cases
76,008 total deaths
46.7% mortality rate

Sierra Leone
138,709 total cases
38,252 total deaths
27.6% mortality rate

Source: 2023 Ebola Global Watch and Global Alert and Response, World Health Organization (WHO)

WEST AFRICA
EBOLA OUTBREAK

Today's internet-driven world provides unprecedented levels of visibility into current events including those that negatively impact human life. Before the internet, we were largely blind to the suffering from natural disasters, war and widespread disease. But now, these tragic stories can be effectively communicated by incorporating data that quantifies human suffering. The more data we share, the more people know. The more people know, the more people get involved and potentially influence policies that change the way these issues are handled.

Global health organizations often lead this charge, but they need insights into specific events and diseases that plague communities. As an example, this dashboard depicts the Ebola outbreak of 2014 in West Africa. As we approached the data set, our goal was to help answer questions for someone unaware of the outbreak's details. Which countries were most affected? How did the outbreak intensify over time? How many people were infected? How many died?

These questions are nearly impossible to answer without data. Answers are even more difficult to communicate. However, time filters at the top help users analyze the outbreak month by month. As months are selected, the map changes dynamically to show how the outbreak affected countries differently. Users can also adjust the map to display either Ebola cases or deaths. The lower three charts compare the three most impacted countries over time, showing outbreak levels for both cases and deaths.

Finally, a journalism narrative appears in the center and gives additional information about the outbreak and how public health agencies responded. The concepts deployed in this dashboard are applicable to many organizations that seek to educate large audiences about tragic events. Data visualizations like these, if paired with a blog or written narrative, help visual learners engage with the information.

Visualizing the increase of Ebola cases and deaths over time is central to this data story and vital to telling it with **integrity**. Users will best understand the rapid outbreak by slicing the data by months. This reinforces the dramatic increase of cases between April and May of 2014.

The top date filter establishes **flow** from left to right. That momentum continues as users analyze country-level impact, working downward to the three charts along the bottom. The *Washington Post* excerpt draws a user's focus back to center, thus anchoring the visuals.

The chaotic, abstract art is incorporated into the title and guides this dashboard's **color**. While the graphic image itself doesn't hold any particular significance, its two colors, red and blue, are used to highlight key metrics: Ebola cases and deaths. Solid black is used in contrast and draws users to other areas with key metrics.

Aa The Franklin **typeface** is used for the title as its large block letters reinforce the urgent nature of the Ebola outbreak. The title also appears oversized and vertical, giving this dashboard unique character. The other dashboard text appears in Segoe, which provides contrast with the title's font and allows users to focus on content.

The abstract art image is a unique element and brings **charm** to the design. It reinforces the disjointed nature of the world's response to the Ebola outbreak. Country icons help organize a country-level analysis at the bottom of the dashboard. These design elements make this dashboard easily identifiable and memorable.

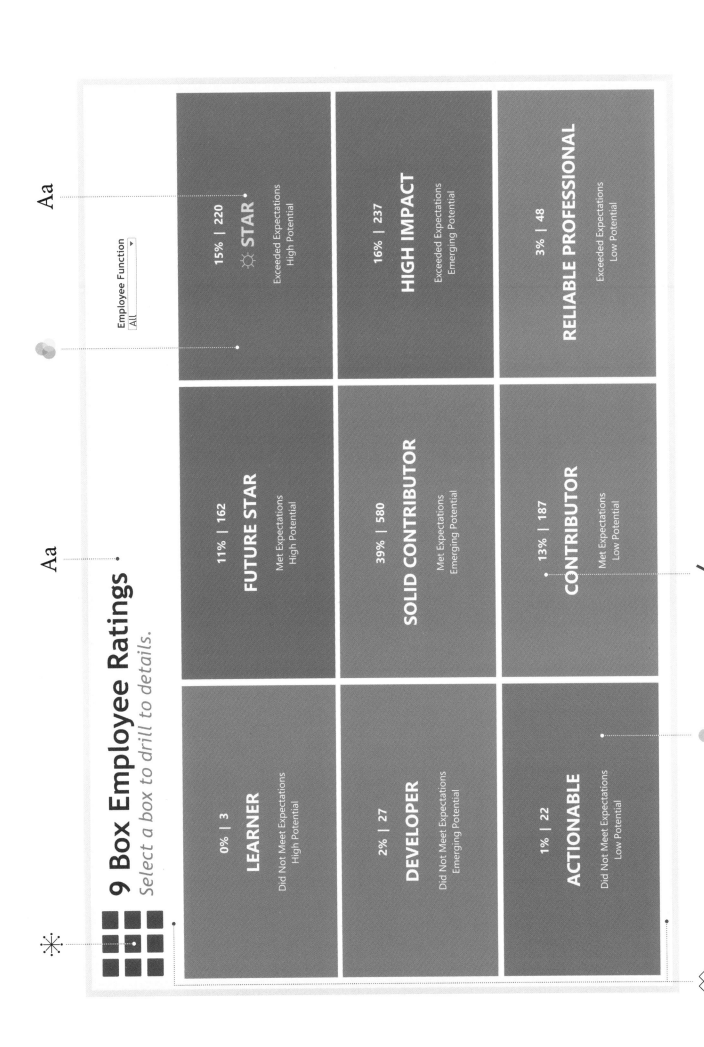

9 Box Employee Ratings
Select a box to drill to details.

Employee Function
All

LEARNER 0% | 3 Did Not Meet Expectations High Potential	**FUTURE STAR** 11% | 162 Met Expectations High Potential	**STAR** ☼ 15% | 220 Exceeded Expectations High Potential
DEVELOPER 2% | 27 Did Not Meet Expectations Emerging Potential	**SOLID CONTRIBUTOR** 39% | 580 Met Expectations Emerging Potential	**HIGH IMPACT** 16% | 237 Exceeded Expectations Emerging Potential
ACTIONABLE 1% | 22 Did Not Meet Expectations Low Potential	**CONTRIBUTOR** 13% | 187 Met Expectations Low Potential	**RELIABLE PROFESSIONAL** 3% | 48 Exceeded Expectations Low Potential

The human resources field is riddled with unknowns. What motivates employees? What contributes to someone's decision to leave a job? To stay? Research suggests that employee behavior is predictable. Many organizations pay close attention to flight risk factors in hopes of understanding the driving force behind an employee's choice to stay or go. HR leadership also depends on key metrics about employee engagement to evaluate behavior and make important decisions about anything from promotions to layoffs.

This dashboard leverages the commonly used HR nine box. The simple three-by-three grid will be familiar to most HR professionals. It organizes employees based on performance and potential. While the traditional nine box is helpful for high-level analysis, it leaves questions on the table. What employees are represented in each section? How do employees compare to each other? What key metrics are contributing to employee distribution in the nine box?

This updated and interactive version not only shows the number of employees in each segment but also allows users to click that grid square and learn more about the associated employees. The second, more detailed dashboard, not pictured here, segments employees into risk levels and measures the associated impact if those employees are not retained. Users get increasingly detailed information as they move down the dashboard, which includes information about an employee's hire date, length in current position, most recent nine box ranking, and compa-ratio.

While organizations pay attention to different measures, there are usually employee-level metrics that help human resource professionals make the best decisions possible. A dynamic nine box like this one allows a human resources organization to focus on measures most important to them and their business.

Listing the actual number of employees together with the percentage of employees as they relate to each grid section's rating gives this dashboard added **integrity**. Without both values, users would not be able to easily quantify a percentage with the number of individuals represented in that percentage.

This dashboard's **flow** is extremely versatile. Users can move through the nine box in any direction to locate the information needed. The simple design, which leverages an industry convention, facilitates the flexibility to answer a wide variety of questions about human resource related activities.

Color highlights the poles of employee distribution. High-performing employees are indicated in blue; disengaged employees in red. Key decisions about promotions or layoffs often involve employees in those two groups. In contrast, average performers are indicated in gray.

The Segoe **typeface** is used throughout this dashboard. It's a great alternative to other san serif fonts because it's functional for professional dashboards but also more contemporary. Also, text size helps emphasize key metrics. The largest text size is allocated to the employees group based on their performance and potential.

Leveraging a conventional grid alone gives this dashboard **charm**. Users find a familiar looking tool but are drawn in by added functionality and interaction. Additionally, the three-by-three icon in the upper left corner reflects the structure of this dashboard and adds design value.

33

GAMEDAY attendance

THE DECISIVE DATA UNIVERSITY ATHLETICS TICKET OFFICE | (206) 747 6930

Decisive Data University — 75

East Austin — 69

	Revenue Collected	Sold Tickets
	$683,008	8,004
	Uncollected Revenue	Unsold Tickets
	$340,992	3,996

Attendance %

66%

Attendance % by Game
vs. average

100%
80%
60%
40%

11/1/15 12/1/15 1/1/16 2/1/16 3/1/16

Stadium Attendance *select a section to see detail*

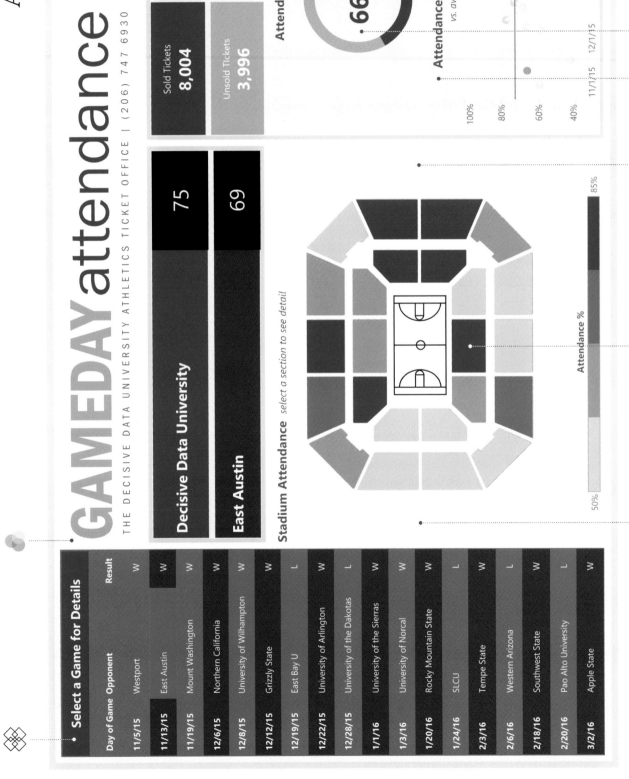

Attendance %

50% 85%

Select a Game for Details

Day of Game	Opponent	Result
11/5/15	Westport	W
11/13/15	East Austin	W
11/19/15	Mount Washington	W
12/6/15	Northern California	W
12/8/15	University of Wilhampton	W
12/12/15	Grizzly State	W
12/19/15	East Bay U	L
12/22/15	University of Arlington	W
12/28/15	University of the Dakotas	L
1/1/16	University of the Sierras	W
1/3/16	University of Norcal	W
1/20/16	Rocky Mountain State	W
1/24/16	SLCU	L
2/3/16	Tempe State	W
2/6/16	Western Arizona	L
2/18/16	Southwest State	W
2/20/16	Pao Alto University	L
3/2/16	Apple State	W

Aa

Aa

INTERCOLLEGIATE ATHLETICS

STADIUM SEATING

Behind every winning college basketball team is a healthy bottom line. As college sports increase in popularity, athletic departments across the country rely on data to help them identify trends that maximize revenue. Is there a correlation between a win streak and high ticket sales? Do specific sections in an arena sell better? How do individual game revenues compare to the season's average?

Fans may not always think about these questions, but the answers are paramount to a revenue-generating athletic organization. Collecting data and visualizing it helps an athletic department maximize ticket sales for high-demand sports, like football and basketball, in order to support less popular sports, like swimming and track.

This dashboard focuses on ticket sales for a college basketball season. The game schedule is listed on the far left and resembles the familiar format. The title, "GameDay Attendance," also identifies the type of data being analyzed. As games are selected on the left, the dashboard updates to show key metrics about each game. When no games are selected, the default view displays values summarized for the entire season.

The central visual is the seating map. Divided sections show how they differ in occupancy from game to game. This information is valuable when determining section pricing. Further to the right, users see high-level revenue metrics for each game as well as uncollected revenue from unsold tickets.

Using data to understand demand for any commodity, including a game ticket, is vital to adjusting prices and maximizing profits. These concepts are highly transferable to other fields that experience volatility in supply and demand.

 The arena map, which shows attendance by section, adds **integrity** by providing an opportunity for more granular analysis of occupancy. Including opponent, final score, and game date provides additional context that might impact sales. Integrity means including this information to enable more meaningful analysis.

 The arena map establishes the **flow** to the center of this dashboard. The left column provides a starting place and functions as a filter to dynamically change the entire dashboard. Momentum moves into the map from the left filter and progresses to the right column for more granular data based on user selections.

 Purple and orange were used to correspond with this university's school **colors**. On the arena map, sections are colored in different shades of purple to indicate attendance percentage and give a quick comparison of sections based on attendance. Sequential color palettes are often the best choice when negative values don't exist. Finally, single games with above-average attendance are called out using dark purple in the trend chart.

Aa Franklin and Segoe **typefaces** appear on this dashboard. The decorative title reinforces the spirit of sporting events and aligns with university branding. All text in the body of this dashboard is a modern, sans-serif typeface. Headers and predominant information are distinguished by bolded text, while labels and supplementary information appear in a faint gray.

 This dashboard oozes **charm**. At the center of it is the arena map, a custom-made visual that speaks directly to both the athletics industry and the university itself. Users identify the subject matter instantly through their universal connection to sports.

35

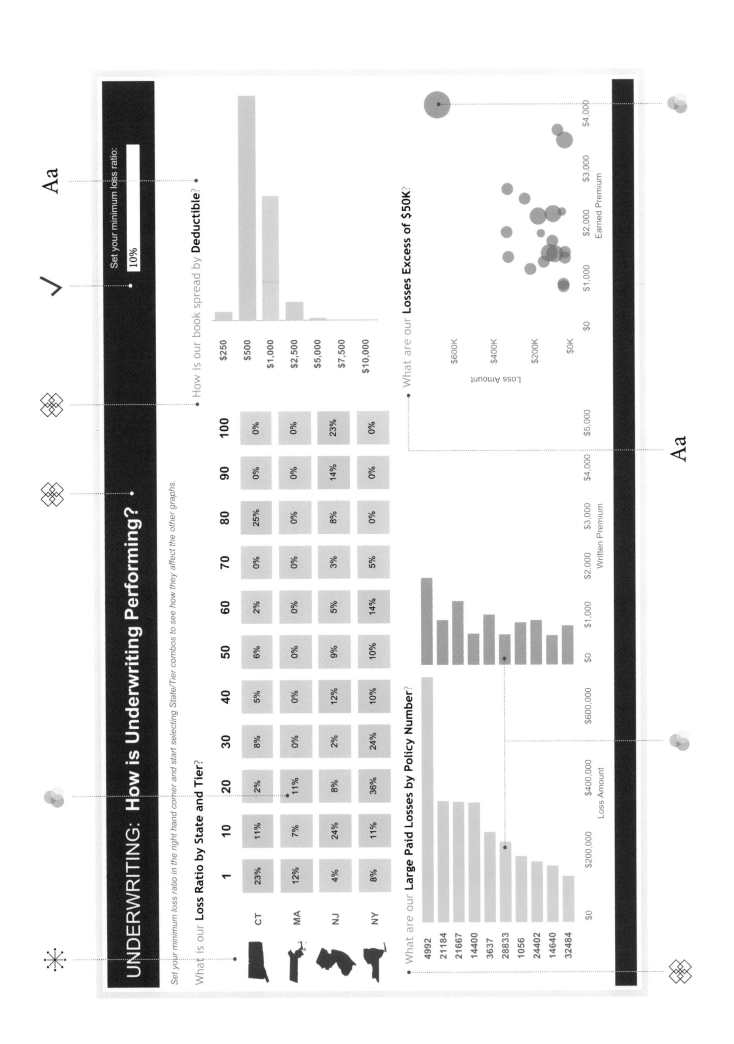

INSURANCE
UNDERWRITING

Homeowner's insurance can be a life saver when the unexpected pops up. Insurance companies use premium payments from policyholders to fix or rebuild any damages a property incurs. They also rely on premiums to make a profit. At the core of the insurance industry is the loss ratio; a single metric that indicates the health of a company and book spread. Put simply, it is a balance of money going out (losses) versus money coming in (earned premiums).

Insurance companies must identify "bad risks," i.e., a policy that is much more likely to lose money than to make money. They do this by putting homes into different categories called Tiers. In a Tier 100, for example, the homeowner probably has every risk mitigation strategy implemented, lives in a safe neighborhood, and has a structure made of sturdy material. Conversely, a Tier 1 falls on the other end of the spectrum.

So what does this dashboard tell users? First, in comparison to the rest of its book, New York is a losing proposition with a greater loss ratio than any another state. Similarly, Tier 10 is a loss leader and we would benefit from doing less business that falls into this Tier. Lastly, its $1,000 deductible business is booming. It is a large portion of its book spread, but also maintains one of the lowest loss ratios driving profit for the company.

Ultimately, an underwriter can use this information to write less losing business and write more winning business. If the goal is to mitigate losses, users can quickly identify through this set of visuals where and who is most likely to have a loss.

 While loss ratio is the primary metric in this dashboard, it can be deceiving since it is a ratio of two numbers. The actual loss amount and associated premium are included where possible to give a sense of the magnitude of the loss. Including both of these metrics is important to telling this story with **integrity**.

 The State and Tier graph establishes the **flow** of this dashboard, which is strongly based on the hierarchy of a policy. Each policy can be categorized by state or tier, then by deductible, and, finally, by the actual policy number itself. Dashboard flow will guide users through all these tiers and facilitate a thorough analysis.

 Color highlights areas of the business that are above a chosen loss ratio. Anything that falls below this minimum is muted in gray, while those that exceed this minimum are highlighted in orange, which evokes urgency. Blue is used as a neutral and is unaffected by the parameter.

Aa The **typeface** chosen is consistently Arial. Given that most of the information is based on currency, Arial is a logical choice as the font allows for a simple and clean reading and alignment of all numbers. The title appears in all caps to differentiate it from the rest of the dashboard.

 State shapes are used in conjunction with the states' abbreviated initials. Not only is this cleaner, but it also gives users an immediately recognizable image. As a general rule, users engage more when they get more visual data with less need to read. Visual communication is just one example of **charm**.

INVESTMENT CALCULATOR

What if you invested

enter original investment amount
$100.00

back on

enter date (weekday)
5/18/2015

?

Select View
Historical Trend ▼

Select company(s) to invest in
All ▼

click to filter

Original shares on May.18.11
2.316

Value on Dec.31.15
▲ **$167.81**

Gain/Loss %
▲ **67.8%**

Gain/Loss $
+**$67.81**

AAPL
Apple
▲ 132.8%

AXP
American Express Co.
▲ 44.5%

BA
Boeing Co.
▲ 108.2%

BAC
Bank of America
▲ 47.3%

CAT
Caterpillar Inc.
▼ -27.2%

CSCO
Cisco Systems
▲ 83.6%

money is evenly split between companies

80

70

60

50

40

30

20

10

0

Mar'11   Sep'11   Mar'12   Sep'12   Mar'13   Sep'13   Mar'14   Sep'14   Mar'15   Sep'15   Mar'16

Aa

INVESTMENT CALCULATOR

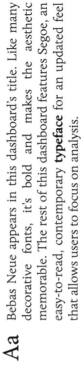

Anyone who has delved into the world of personal investing knows that anguish and elation can be part of the experience. Investing in stocks can be a very lucrative investment strategy. It's also very high risk. While it's impossible to know how a stock will grow and trend moving forward, stock market data lends some insight into what might happen. When investors can analyze that data and assess potential outcomes based on different investment strategies, they're better able to understand trends in the stock market.

This dashboard is highly interactive and dynamic. Users can adjust specific investment parameters, such as amount, date and stock. Similar to the stock application on Apple phones, the layout and visuals are compelling and jump off the page. It helps answer key questions like: Which companies have experienced the most volatility? What would be a good diversification approach across several industries?

At first glance, this dashboard does nothing more than highlight missed opportunities. So, how is this helpful today? Suppose a $100 investment in Apple five years ago yielded a 100% return? Wouldn't that information impact future investments? Historical price increases do not guarantee future health, but history has a tendency to repeat itself. A working knowledge of what has occurred at least gives an investor more context.

Integrity is maintained with a data model that enables users to simulate a specific investment in an easy and efficient manner. From an analytical integrity perspective, users have the option to select a historical trend that provides more context into the investment gain projections.

The filter at the top directs users to input parameters that control the trend chart. It leverages one color to create a cohesive **flow** between input and output. Momentum is maintained as users move from the main visual trend to individual stock performance tiles on the right.

Color is used as a visual engagement cue to highlight interactivity. The red and green palette is indicative of the classic gain/loss colors traditionally used in the stock market. The blues are decorative, but functional, as they contrast and complement with the reds and greens.

Aa

Bebas Neue appears in this dashboard's title. Like many decorative fonts, it's bold and makes the aesthetic memorable. The rest of this dashboard features Segoe, an easy-to-read, contemporary **typeface** for an updated feel that allows users to focus on analysis.

✳

The trend chart icon to the right of the title helps identify the data topic immediately and mirrors the very prominent histogram that invites users to engage with this dashboard. Subtle growth/decline arrows within the summary tiles at the far right also provide **charm** through visual communication.

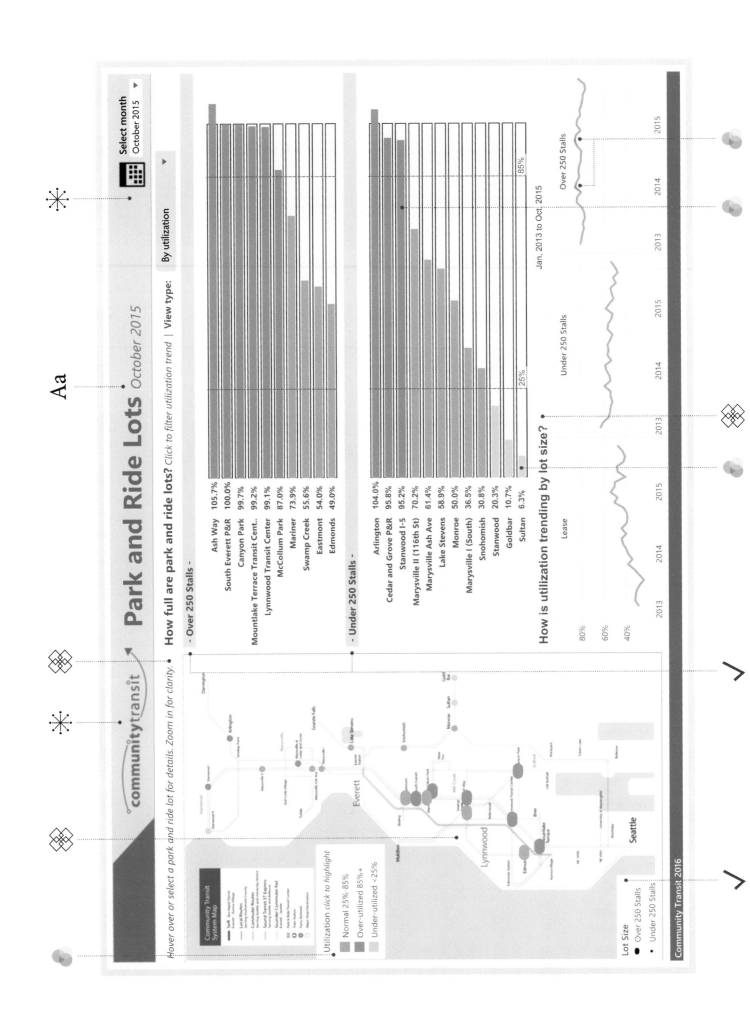

Park and Ride Lots *October 2015*

Select month
October 2015 ▼

How full are park and ride lots? *Click to filter utilization trend* | **View type:** By utilization

Hover over or select a park and ride lot for details. Zoom in for clarity.

- Over 250 Stalls -

Ash Way	105.7%
South Everett P&R	100.0%
Canyon Park	99.7%
Mountlake Terrace Transit Cent..	99.2%
Lynnwood Transit Center	99.1%
McCollum Park	87.0%
Mariner	73.9%
Swamp Creek	55.6%
Eastmont	54.0%
Edmonds	49.0%

- Under 250 Stalls -

Arlington	104.0%
Cedar and Grove P&R	95.8%
Stanwood I-5	95.2%
Marysville II (116th St)	70.2%
Marysville Ash Ave	61.4%
Lake Stevens	58.9%
Monroe	50.0%
Marysville I (South)	36.5%
Snohomish	30.8%
Stanwood	20.3%
Goldbar	10.7%
Sultan	6.3%

85%

25%

Community Transit System Map

Swift — Blue, Seaport Transit, Everett – Aurora Village
Local Routes — Serving Snohomish County
Commuter Routes — Serving Snohomish and University District
Sound Transit ST Express — Serving Seattle and Bellevue
Sounder Commuter Rail — Everett – Seattle
Park & Ride/Transit Center
Train Station
Ferry Terminal
Major Stop/Destination

Utilization click to highlight

Normal 25% 85%
Over-utilized 85%+
Under-utilized <25%

How is utilization trending by lot size?

Jan. 2013 to Oct. 2015

Under 250 Stalls

Over 250 Stalls

Lease

80%
60%
40%

2013 2014 2015
2013 2014 2015
2014 2015

Lot Size
● Over 250 Stalls
● Under 250 Stalls

PARK AND RIDE USAGE

Community Transit is a service-based company that has become a leader for providing public transportation options for Seattle and the surrounding areas. The park and ride lots that it operates provide commuters easy access to major bus routes. The leadership team has an increasing desire to know how well the park and ride lots are being utilized in order to increase public utility.

Lot utilization percentage is the key metric in this dashboard. Users can hover over the map to highlight the bars and learn more about a particular lot and area. By clicking into a bar, users filter utilization trends. At the top right, a dynamic parameter switches between totals and utilization percentage views, providing even more detail. Compelling tooltips provide yet additional granular detail for users.

The tremendous flexibility of these visuals helps explain which lots require more active management, such as supervising direct traffic flow, monitoring parking violations and/or maintaining pay machines. Visualizations also help evaluate over-utilized lots needing expansion or under-utilized lots that may need to be closed. As an example, we can see that lots along the I-5 corridor need more stalls. With these insights, users can discuss whether that means expanding or adding lots.

Service-based companies, like Community Transit, can leverage the highly dynamic and detailed data illustrated here to develop a clear path for where to focus their efforts. They can also consider the possibility and practicality of downsizing or lowering their level of service within outlying regions of their service areas.

Utilization percentage is clearly represented, but without the ability to also see totals, users wouldn't have any information and perspective on lot size differences. This functionality to switch between 'totals' and 'utilization' percentage tells a complete story and improves **integrity**. Also, users can separate out lots based on size, which encourages comparison within appropriate lot size groups.

The schematic map on the left side establishes **flow**. Users intuitively start at the map, by hovering over map locations, and are then guided to the detailed bar charts. From the bar charts, users can filter out a park and ride lot on the trend line.

The soft, pastel **color** scheme plays off the pre-determined aesthetics of the map provided by the client. A custom sequential color palette ties the visuals together by reinforcing set thresholds for normal, under and over. Red creates urgency and highlights over-utilization. Yellow is secondary to red, highlighting lots that are under-utilized.

The **typeface** used in this dashboard, Segoe, aligns with the organization's brand, which is important for continuity. Although the same font style is consistent throughout, some creative liberties were taken with the title in the form of font size and color to add a bit of variance.

This dashboard's custom map is the strongest example of **charm**. Its aesthetic is specific to Community Transit, but also follows conventional transit map design. Community Transit's brand and logo adds even more charm, and a calendar icon draws the user's eye to the month filter and visually communicates its purpose.

Billy Reynolds · | RHP | Decisive Data Developers

pitch location heat map

84,986
pitches

89.10
avg. speed

PITCHf/x

Pitcher Team
All ▶

Batter Team
All ▶

Pitcher
Baxter Brown ▶

Batter
All ▶

Throws
R   L

Stands
L
R

Count

0-0	1-0	2-0	3-0
0-1	1-1	2-1	3-1
0-2	1-2	2-2	3-2

Pitch Type
- Changeup
- Curveball
- Fastball
- Sinker
- Slider

Pitch Result
- In play
- Called Strike
- Swinging Strike
- Foul
- Ball
- Hit By Pitch

Year
'08 '09 '10 '11 '12 '13 '14 '15 '16

powered by

number of pitches in area
1   585

Fastball	49%
Changeup	16%
Slider	15%
Curveball	10%
Sinker	10%

batter chase %
17.5%

strike %
64.7%

Aa

SPORTS ANALYTICS

PITCHf/x
PLAYER ANALYSIS

Sports analytics explore in depth the numbers surrounding a given sport. Stats and figures that break down an individual game, a season, a team or a player are meticulously recorded to satisfy the super-fan's interest in details. Fans delight in the ability to learn all there is to know about their favorite team and understand developments or challenges their favorite player faces over time. Sports analytics provide a historical narrative for a fan's favorite pastime and a way to be included in the drama of athletics.

There are multiple different users who consume recorded sports data. Sports television, as well as print and on-line media, rely on this information to analyze games, rank players, and provide season overviews. The sports industry uses data to engage fans and inform athletics professionals. Sports teams themselves rely on in-depth analytics to better understand their strategies, allowing coaches and managers, for example, to trade players, optimize field time, and develop a starting lineup.

This dashboard looks at the performance of a selected pitcher in Major League Baseball and displays a thorough analysis of pitches thrown over time. On the left side, users find a number of filters that help to investigate how the selected pitcher performs against a selected team or individual batter. Users can also evaluate right- versus left-handed batters.

The large visualization to the right leverages the conventional strike zone used by the league. As filters are selected on the left, the visualization of pitches changes dynamically and displays the pitches thrown for that cross-section of data. It even provides a breakdown of pitch types and a percentage distribution for the pitcher. All this information becomes very useful for a pitcher's coach, manager and opposing batters.

A sports-related data story like this one exemplifies the power of data analytics and the impact they can have on everyone who's interested. Fans gain the detail they crave about their favorite teams, journalists gain the content needed to thoroughly report on athletics, and sports teams gain useful information to make data-driven business decisions.

 The upper right corner displays the total number of pitches in the data set for the selected pitcher. It provides **integrity** by reminding users to consider the volume of pitches as they analyze the stats. Without knowing how much data exists for each selected pitcher, users wouldn't have an accurate and complete picture for analysis.

 The upper left-hand corner, which contains the filters necessary for in-depth analysis, sets this dashboard's **flow**. This strategic design conforms with conventional left-to-right reading structures and establishes a natural momentum. After filters are selected, the flow moves to the right where users see the large, dynamic visualization.

 A blue-to-orange gradient is used to showcase volume of pitches. Orange emphasizes areas of high-pitch volume more than those with a low-pitch volume because the bold **color** contrasts more with the charcoal background than blue does. This strategic choice allows users to focus on a pitcher's most common strike zone. This dark background palette further helps the selected colors stand out.

 Because this dashboard uses many custom images and visual themes that reinforce the subject, a simple **typeface,** like Segoe, is used throughout so as not to distract. Large, bold text is used to highlight key metrics without distracting from the graphics.

 This dashboard has **charm** at every turn that identifies the subject to users. The left side displays icons for left- and right-hand batters as well as small baseball icons for pitch type and result. The large, right-side visualization features two contour batters (also representing left- and right-hand batters) that provide reference for the strike zone and an engaging, almost "live motion" graphic.

43

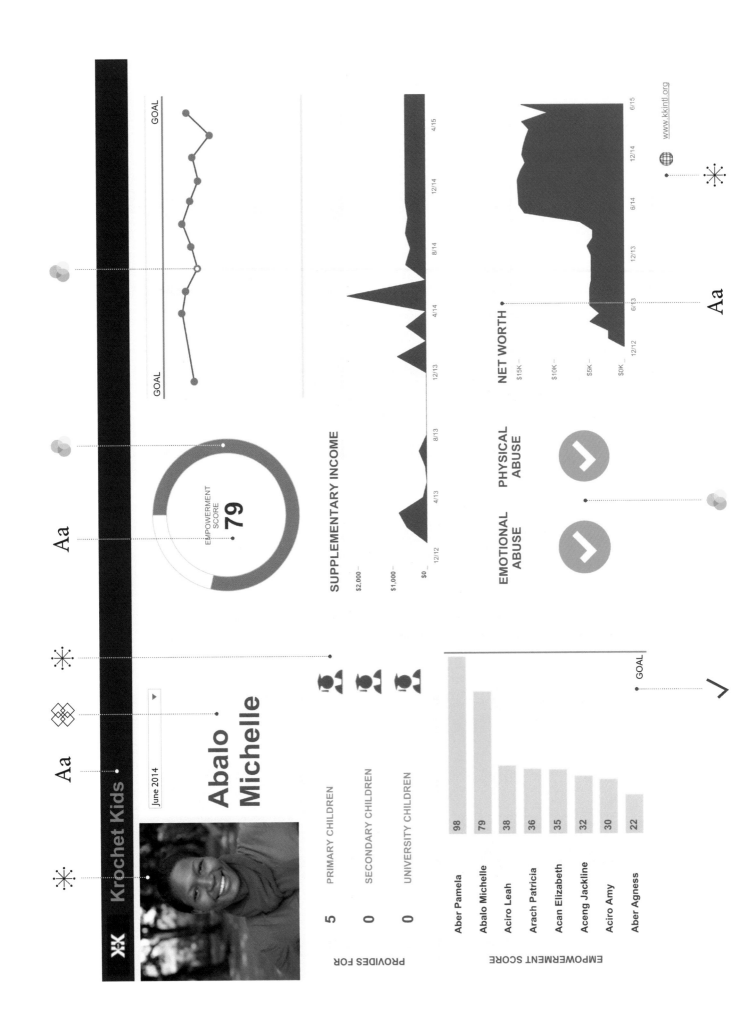

Krochet Kids

June 2014

Abalo Michelle

PROVIDES FOR

5 PRIMARY CHILDREN

0 SECONDARY CHILDREN

0 UNIVERSITY CHILDREN

GOAL   GOAL

EMPOWERMENT SCORE
79

SUPPLEMENTARY INCOME

$2,000
$1,000
$0

12/12   4/13   8/13   12/13   4/14   8/14   12/14   4/15

EMOTIONAL ABUSE   PHYSICAL ABUSE

NET WORTH

$15K
$10K
$5K
$0K

12/12   6/13   12/13   6/14   12/14   6/15

EMPOWERMENT SCORE

Aber Pamela	98
Abalo Michelle	79
Aciro Leah	38
Arach Patricia	36
Acan Elizabeth	35
Aceng Jackline	32
Aciro Amy	30
Aber Agness	22

GOAL

www.kkintl.org

Aa

KROCHET KIDS
SOCIAL IMPACT

Data is more critical to measuring success than ever before for non-profits. As organizations offer more comprehensive reporting on their relief efforts, donors grow to expect organizations to account for their received donations. Supporters of these organizations want to know whether or not their donations are making an impact.

Krochet Kids is an innovative non-profit that empowers women in Peru and Uganda to rise above poverty by creating and selling handmade apparel and crocheted hats. The organization has several donors who help support a portion of the operations and want to know exactly how the women are being empowered and impacted. With an algorithm that aggregates nearly 50 metrics, each woman in the program is given a monthly "empowerment score," which considers both quantitative measures and qualitative factors to define health.

The top left of this dashboard displays a woman's profile and a month's snapshot according to selection. Users can navigate to the bottom left corner and change the display to another profile. This also provides context into how each woman is doing compared to the other women in the program from an empowerment perspective. The top four metrics, which include supplementary income trends, emotional abuse, physical abuse and net worth, provide insight into the well being and overall empowerment of each woman.

This kind of data exposure and diagnostic display will be increasingly critical to the health of non-profits in the future. Donors will not only feel a connection to the women who they are partnering with, they'll be more confident that their funds are being directed towards life changing work. The impact is huge. Donors and volunteers will have far greater desire and comfort in contributing in large capacity.

 The context of the trend line shows the improvement or decline of the empowerment score over time. Without this trend line and historical insight, users would not fully understand the context of a woman's story and the program's impact on her. Providing historical data rather than solely focusing on a current state, improves **integrity** and tells a more complete story.

 When we think of social impact, we usually start with the person behind the numbers. For that reason, a photograph holder for the women is positioned in the top left-hand corner. This establishes **flow** by drawing users in and emphasizing the individual impacted by the non-profit.

 Color is used sparingly in this dashboard. Red, a powerful color, indicates progress towards 100% empowerment. Green, a color often associated with health, indicates that a woman is meeting health standards in the areas of emotional or physical abuse. Supporting metrics are displayed in a neutral gray to avoid over-emphasizing less critical measures.

Aa This dashboard uses Arial, which is a simple **typeface** and allows users to focus on the photo instead of decorative titles. The font size helps humanize this dashboard by enlarging the woman's name over that of the company itself. This is a deliberate effort to highlight the organization's mission: individual female empowerment. A woman's empowerment score also appears larger in size to emphasize this dashboard's main measure.

 The overall **charm** of this dashboard is in the way data and design have been highly personalized. Profiles appear in the top left, which include an engaging image of the individual, adding warmth and relatability. Additionally, a subtle black header with Krochet Kids' logo is featured at the top to reinforce branding.

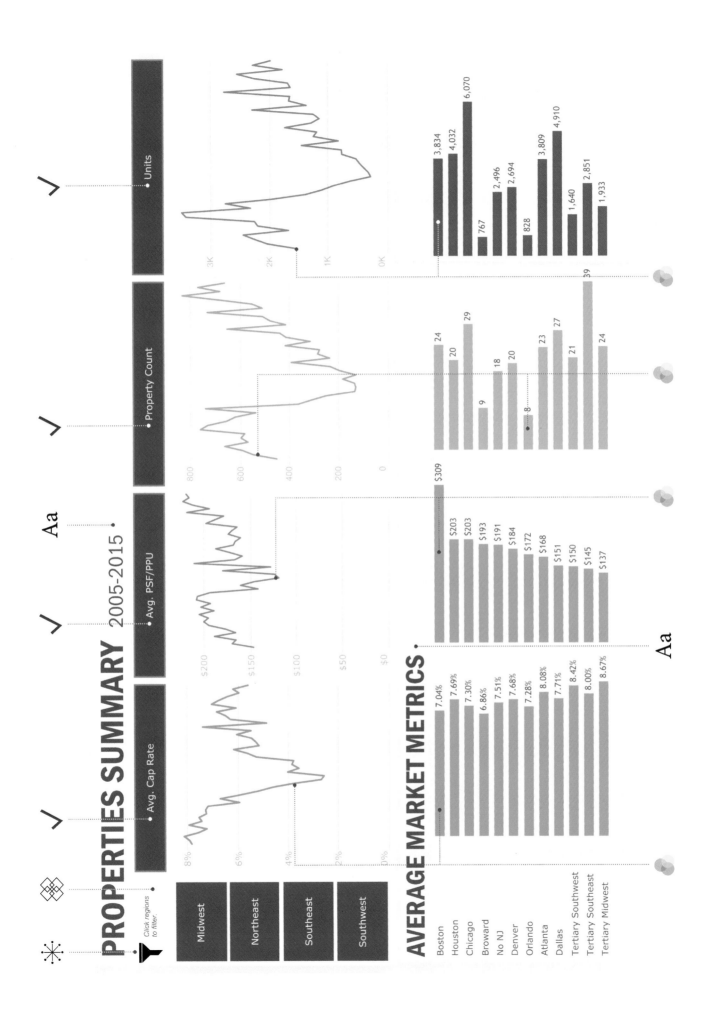

NATIONAL PROPERTY SNAPSHOT

Real estate investment executives are constantly analyzing trends to predict downturns and potential upticks in the housing marketplace, ultimately to measure the health of their investment portfolio. To gain these insights, they must review several sources, which takes significant time. Questions include: How have top metric indicators performed over a period of time? Does this give us an advantage to predict what might happen next? Which markets have the most potential growth? Are we leveraging our capital in the appropriate markets?

This dashboard helps answer these questions. High-level metrics with the ability to drill into one of four regions—down to a specific market—give users a tool to quickly understand a portfolio's performance. Average cap rate, average price per square foot, property count, and number of units are all key metrics that are being trended over the past 10 years. They give insight into overall performance. Side-by-side trend lines make correlations easy to identify. Peaks and valleys stand out, urging users to drill into the details of a specific month to see which markets were producing out of the ordinary results. Finally, bar charts along the bottom provide a direct comparison between markets. They address questions like: Which markets should we continue to invest in or pull out of?

Executives are extremely busy and rely on quick insights into the performance of their business and/or portfolio. Such intuitive filtering, small multiple trend lines, and simple visuals like bar charts, greatly help users take action and move their business forward.

Four key metrics are used in a similar visual to provide overall health of a portfolio, which gives a more robust picture and improves **integrity**. Likewise, averages are used in trend lines to provide context for how cities and areas compare. Providing both city actuals and historical averages gives more analytical integrity to the story.

Flow moves downward. Users see the filter at the top left first and then move to overall health over the past 10 years. The lower visualization also provides a more detailed view into market comparisons.

A cool **color** palette reflects the natural hues of this company's Pacific Northwest roots. A separate color is assigned to each of this dashboard's four key metrics, allowing them to stand out individually. Filters and headers are designated by a neutral, dark gray, lending more attention to the data story.

Aa A decorative, bold **typeface**, Franklin, is used to separate high-level and granular data. Franklin fonts like this one are contemporary and help this dashboard feel up-to-date and relevant. In addition, the font size becomes smaller with increased granularity, which is a visual clue reminding users they are analyzing city-specific data.

Rather than using default dropdown filters on the left side, custom tiled filters were created to add more **charm**. Additionally, a small filter icon helps bring visual attention to the tiles, clearly indicating where to start.

CRIME RATES: EAST HUNTSVILLE 2011-2012

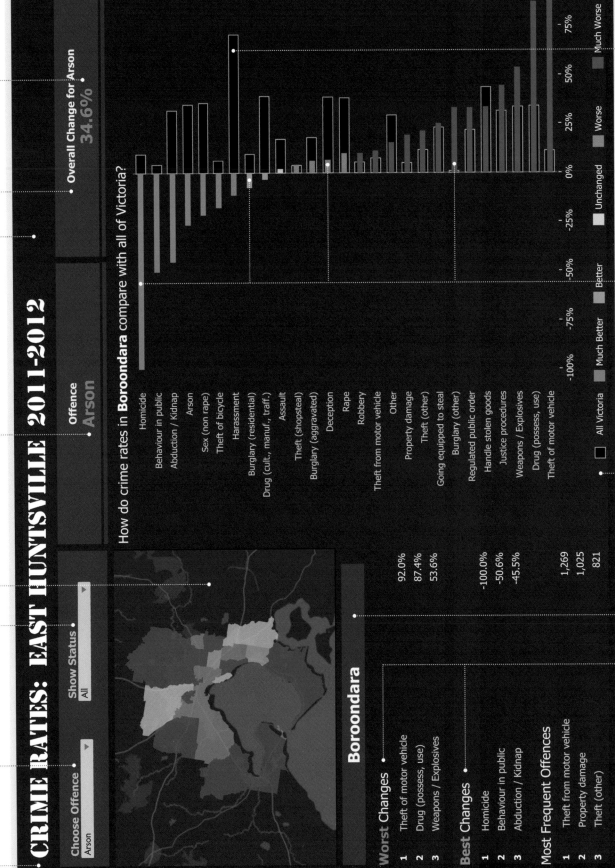

Choose Offence
Arson

Show Status
All

Offence
Arson

Overall Change for Arson
34.6%

How do crime rates in **Boroondara** compare with all of Victoria?

Homicide
Behaviour in public
Abduction / Kidnap
Arson
Sex (non rape)
Theft of bicycle
Harassment
Burglary (residential)
Drug (cult., manuf., traff.)
Assault
Theft (shopsteal)
Burglary (aggravated)
Deception
Rape
Robbery
Theft from motor vehicle
Other
Property damage
Theft (other)
Going equipped to steal
Burglary (other)
Regulated public order
Handle stolen goods
Justice procedures
Weapons / Explosives
Drug (possess, use)
Theft of motor vehicle

-100% -75% -50% -25% 0% 25% 50% 75% 100%

☐ All Victoria   ■ Much Better   ■ Better   ■ Unchanged   ■ Worse   ■ Much Worse

Boroondara

Worst Changes
1 Theft of motor vehicle   92.0%
2 Drug (possess, use)   87.4%
3 Weapons / Explosives   53.6%

Best Changes
1 Homicide   -100.0%
2 Behaviour in public   -50.6%
3 Abduction / Kidnap   -45.5%

Most Frequent Offences
1 Theft from motor vehicle   1,269
2 Property damage   1,025
3 Theft (other)   821

CRIME REPORTING

CRIME RATES
EAST HUNTSVILLE

Public data on crime rates can help educate citizens and provide insight to governmental agencies and law enforcement. Obviously, the causes of crime are highly complicated, and those areas heavily impacted by crime are often caught up in a vicious cycle of poverty, sub-standard education systems and other difficult problems. But bringing crime rates to the surface can at least foster discussion and help those involved focus their efforts and offer funding to those areas that need it most.

This dashboard of crime rates in East Huntsville clearly identifies these focus areas. From the filters in the top left corner, users can select both an offence and a severity status, which instantly exposes the data for analysis and discovery. The five-stepped color map shows distinct status groups as they compare to East Huntsville's average and an overall view of crime rate health. Other visuals are set to always show one of the areas selected in the map. Additionally, the bottom left panel provides worst changes, best changes and most frequent offences for a high-level understanding. The status selection is close in proximity to the color legend to identify the relationship.

When published for public consumption, crime data can start meaningful conversations about safety and the distribution of public resources. It can even inspire changes to public policy. Publicized, visual analytics have the power to engage communities more than inaccessible data in a warehouse or spreadsheet.

 Because this dashboard evaluates changes in crime rates both at a general level as well as for specific crimes, it makes a thorough analysis and thus achieves **integrity**. This helps users avoid making assumptions about what contributes to crime rates overall. It also helps users evaluate the negative impacts of specific types of crime.

 A top-down, left-right **flow** is established by the placement of the filters and associated map of East Huntsville. The filters are grouped because they impact the entire dashboard and improve user experience.

 Red and blue are used exclusively to indicate negative or positive trends, respectively, and contrast well with the dark, black background. Overall the **colors** invoke an intense theme. Neutralizing colors in the other, less prominent areas of this dashboard, keep the focus on the positives and negatives of key metrics.

 This dashboard's title uses the decorative **typeface** Stencil, a unique, decorative font that reminds users of the 'caution' tape often used at crime scenes. For the remaining text, a font that's less decorative and easier to read is used so as to better engage users with the information.

 Charm is evident in the map layers, which provide a memorable aesthetic and highly interactive component. Again, the intense, dark overall tone suggests a troublesome topic, which reinforces the crime rates data story and helps impress upon users the urgency of the information.

49

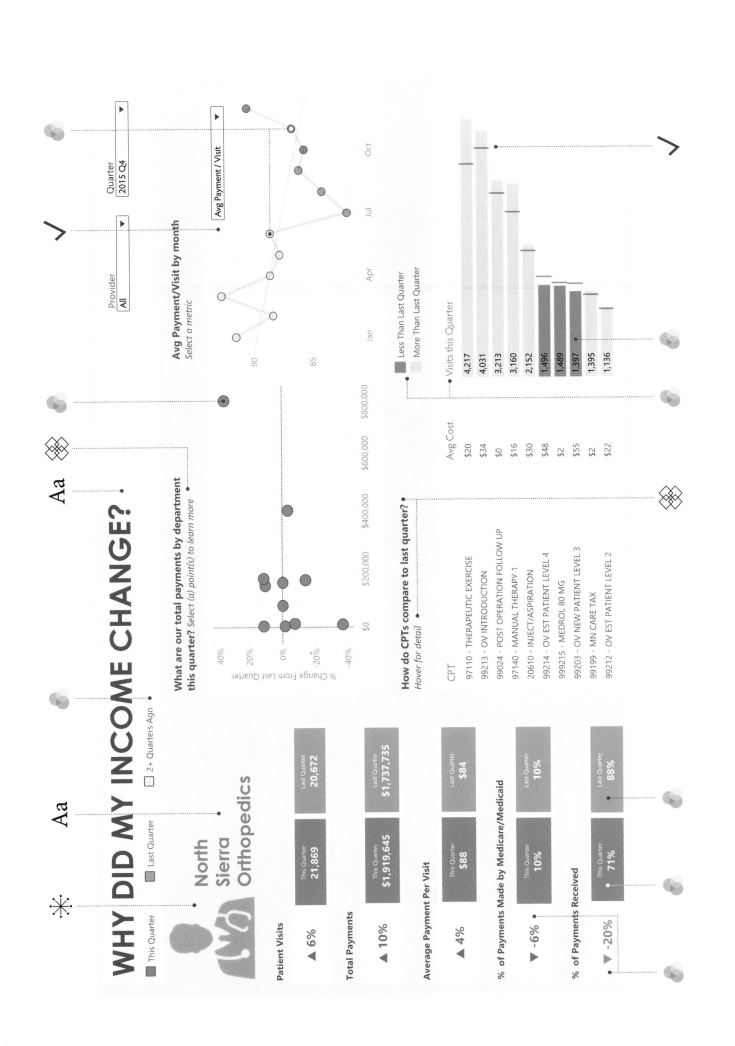

WHY DID MY INCOME CHANGE?

■ This Quarter ■ Last Quarter □ 2+ Quarters Ago

North Sierra Orthopedics

Quarter
2015 Q4 ▼

Provider
All ▼

Avg Payment/Visit by month
Select a metric

Avg Payment / Visit ▼

90

85

Jan   Apr   Jul   Oct

Patient Visits

▲ 6%

This Quarter	Last Quarter
21,869	20,672

Total Payments

▲ 10%

This Quarter	Last Quarter
$1,919,645	$1,737,735

Average Payment Per Visit

▲ 4%

This Quarter	Last Quarter
$88	$84

% of Payments Made by Medicare/Medicaid

▼ -6%

This Quarter	Last Quarter
10%	10%

% of Payments Received

▼ -20%

This Quarter	Last Quarter
71%	88%

What are our total payments by department this quarter? *Select (a) point(s) to learn more*

% Change From Last Quarter

40%
20%
0%
-20%
-40%

$0 $200,000 $400,000 $600,000 $800,000

How do CPTs compare to last quarter?
Hover for detail

■ Less Than Last Quarter
■ More Than Last Quarter

Visits this Quarter

CPT	Avg Cost	
97110 – THERAPEUTIC EXERCISE	$20	4,217
99213 – OV INTRODUCTION	$34	4,031
99024 – POST OPERATION FOLLOW UP	$0	3,213
97140 – MANUAL THERAPY 1	$16	3,160
20610 – INJECT/ASPIRATION	$30	2,152
99214 – OV EST PATIENT LEVEL 4	$48	1,496
999215 – MEDROL 80 MG	$2	1,489
99203 – OV NEW PATIENT LEVEL 3	$55	1,397
99199 – MN CARE TAX	$2	1,395
99212 – OV EST PATIENT LEVEL 2	$22	1,136

PRACTITIONER COMPENSATION

Modifications to Medicare and Medicaid plans have caused healthcare professionals to notice significant changes in their income due to mandated administrative tasks. Usually these professionals only have a gut feeling about these changes because the data is not clear in drawing correlations between the indicators that lead to a drop in pay.

Because time is taken away from seeing patients, hospitals and doctors want a sense of how they performed financially and service-wise across quarters to evaluate what adjustments they might need to make to improve. To answer these questions, healthcare professionals must find correlations between increases/decreases in pay and other metrics such as average payments per visit, Medicare/Medicaid payments and number of patient visits.

This dashboard addresses questions like: Are patient visits trending up or down? What might be causing the decline in patient visits? Are we collecting on payments? Are certain CPTs impacting the hospital's overall performance? Are there departments that are seeing success/failure? What metrics are strong indicators to signal this success/failure? With the provider and quarter filters in the top, right corner, users can dive into granular details. The summary tiles at left draw users into key metrics, signaling overall health. Filtering on a department drives the adjacent trend line with the selected metric and CPT bar chart to answer questions like: Which CPT codes are impacting our key metrics? And in which months was there a dip in any one of the five key metrics?

The healthcare industry has massive amounts of data to analyze. In order to increase patient access to quality care and help healthcare professionals advance their careers, the data must speak to patient volume over time. Patient volume is a key indicator for patient access to care, physician income, and general clinic productivity. For that reason, tracking patient volume quarter to quarter is a key component of analysis.

 Telling this data story with **integrity** means providing a comparison between the current quarter and the last quarter. Displaying data that speaks to only one quarter would hinder any ability to track progress and understand key metric trends.

 The left data pane establishes **flow** by drawing users in to high-level comparisons that show correlations, trends and details to support the high-level numbers on the right. Instructions help guide users, and quick filters at the top right help control and maintain momentum.

 This dashboard uses only two **colors**. Blue is reminiscent of a hospital's interior and highlights the current quarter as the focus. Orange expresses urgency for financial losses and is used sparingly so users can quickly identify declines from last quarter. Using a neutral gray to represent last quarter serves only as a reference.

 This dashboard uses two **typefaces**. Century Gothic provides decorative style to the headers and clinic name. Segoe UI appears elsewhere. This design strategy provides variation to the text and helps users identify key metrics and contextual information.

 The **charm** here is very simple with a physician icon positioned in the upper left corner. Users instantly connect with the subject of this dashboard, making it personal. Also, the contrasting shapes used throughout the display add a subtle charm to the aesthetic.

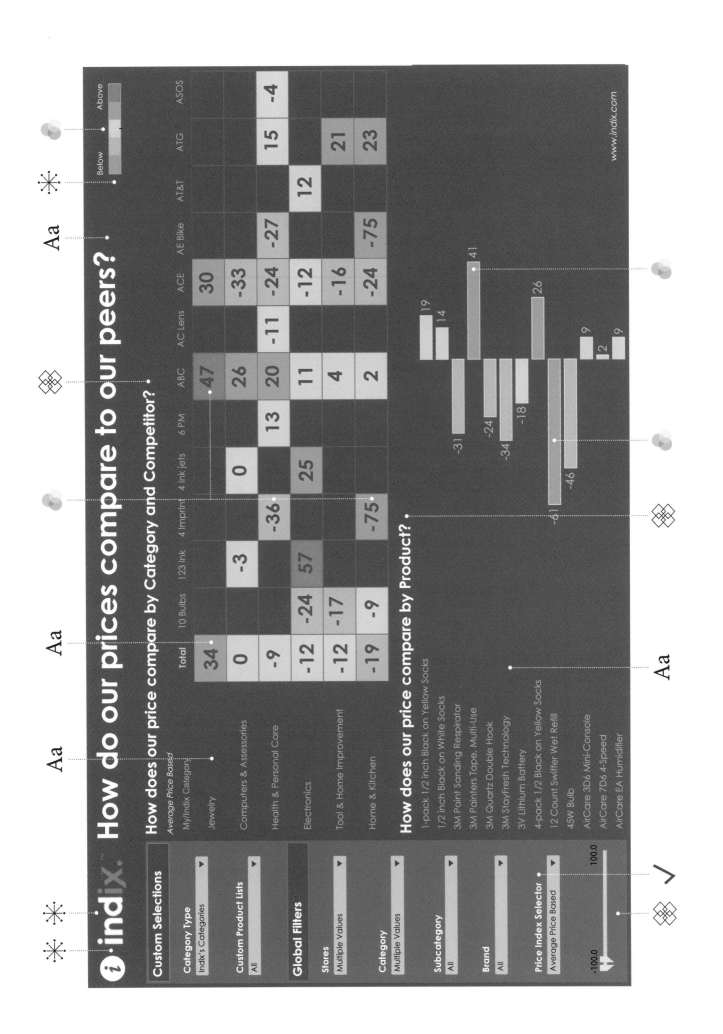

COMPETITIVE PRICING ANALYSIS

Consumers benefit enormously from a market in which multiple vendors sell the same item at difference prices. This is increasingly true with online shopping as more consumers can shop around and find the best deals possible. This highly competitive landscape provides customer savings, but it also presents unique challenges for vendors.

Calibrating sales prices to remain competitive in the market is a daunting task. The constantly changing market for online and in-store sales not only requires vendors to have focused employees but to also be able to record and track competitive prices from tens of thousands of competitors.

This dashboard provides vendors valuable market insight that allows them to appropriately price their goods. For many online retailers who promise a "low price guarantee," the ability to maintain price parity with competitors is integral to their business model. Data, if properly collected and analyzed, can help achieve that.

On the far left, filters are organized into a single column. As users make selections, two major visualizations on the right change dynamically. The top one shows the percent variance of categories for specific competitors. Users can easily identify product categories that are priced too high or too low. They also see an overall percent variance for a given category compared to all competitors.

Price variances by category are important to show how groups of products are priced compared to the market. However, a more granular view of specific products within each category further leverages the data. The lower right visualization itemizes products for all categories. When users select a category from above, the lower list filters to show relevant products and their individual price variance. Users can then identify specific products that contribute to significant category variances. In a time where analyzing big data is increasingly important, succinct and flexible pricing visuals provide the quick insight that sustains a competitive advantage.

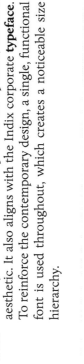

The price index selector improves **integrity** by allowing a flexible comparison based on either a minimum or average price. If users only analyze averages, they wouldn't see how a product's average compares to its minimum price. The price index selector functionality helps show when a product's average dips below the all-time low or when it begins to rise too high compared to its all-time low.

On the left side is an engagement queue for users to filter, which begins the **flow** of this dashboard. On the right, the top-down flow calls out filters that guide users through more granular analysis.

Varying **colors** provide a spectrum to indicate how a product compares with respect to average or minimum price. The blue to red diverging palette (seen by the legend in the upper right corner) helps users identify that relationship. In contrast, titles are white and body text off-white to create visual hierarchy.

Century Gothic is used to provide an updated, modern aesthetic. It also aligns with the Indix corporate **typeface.** To reinforce the contemporary design, a single, functional font is used throughout, which creates a noticeable size hierarchy.

The Indix logo and adjacent information button lend a professional branding and **charm** to this dashboard's overall image. Incorporating that branding imagery makes the dashboard relevant to the company's users and memorable for external users.

STUDENT DEMOGRAPHICS AND PERFORMANCE

Use the map to filter by school district & city
Use the ethnicity chart to filter by ethnicity & grade

● WA Cities ● OR Cities
sized by enrollment

South Sound SCHOOL DISTRICT

Federal Way

STUDENT ETHNICITY BY GRADE

■ African American ■ Asian ■ Caucasian ■ Hispanic ■ Native American

Grade					
10	11%	11%	57%	16%	5%
11	7%	13%	70%	11%	
12	19%	10%	48%	24%	

0%   25%   50%   75%   100%

ENROLLMENT BY MEAL PLAN

No Meal Plan — 71
Lunch Meal Plan — 49
Breakfast Meal Plan — 26
Full Meal Plan — 8

STANDARDIZED TEST SCORES vs STATE AVG

○ State Avg   ● Above State Avg   ● Below State Avg

SCIENCE ‖

MATH -5%

READING +4%

TEACHER EVAL -13%

STUDENT DEMOGRAPHICS & PERFORMANCE

Public schools are continually trying to understand the correlation between demographics and academic performance, which is commonly measured by standardized testing. Test scores are often compared with state averages to gauge performance. Such data begs questions like: What districts have a high population of "x" ethnicity and how does that correlate with standardized testing? Is there a correlation between ethnicity and performance? Do teachers in less populated areas connect better with students, and thus, receive better evaluations?

A fundamental understanding of this information can drive staffing and curriculum decisions. This dashboard allows users to explore school districts within Washington and Oregon and drill down to highly granular levels to compare standardized test scores against the state average scores. Beginning at the map, users can filter by school district and city. City locations are pinpointed by circles, colored by state and sized by enrollment.

Once a district or city is chosen, the visuals on the right update to reveal demographic information and performance versus state average in three core subjects as well as in teacher evaluations. The focus is on student performance at a very granular level. Users can potentially drill down by district, city, grade and ethnicity to then gain quick insight to the selected subset's performance.

Visualizing public education data like this allows users to better engage in conversation about how students are performing. For public schools to improve a student's education, they must make decisions based on comprehensive data that help draw accurate correlations to specific outcomes.

 Because percentages are mostly evaluated in this dashboard, they must be quantified to maintain **integrity**. Therefore, student count is included. Without knowing the raw number of students, users would have no indication of sample size.

 Generally, this dashboard reads left to right and top to bottom, beginning with the interactive map on the left. But given the most critical information is percentages, the test score visual sits in the middle to focus **flow** to the center rather than to the bottom corner.

 A vibrant **color** palette calls out ethnicity groups on the bar charts to provide contrast for the dark background. Different colors are used in the visual below to differentiate the data and drive meaning in the test score visual.

Aa This dashboard uses Franklin. It has a more decorative, updated feel and contrasts with Arial, the **typeface** used throughout other sections. Along with using different fonts, varying text sizes in the headers adds to the nuance of the graphic design.

 Charm is subtle in this dashboard. The map background dissolves into the right side providing a seamless finish. The filter icon beside the collection of school districts cues users to modify the display. Finally, the test score circle-in-circle visual is sized by score, showing a creative way to compare scores with averages.

SUMMARY

A t Decisive Data, our mission is to help people use data to realize better outcomes. Our consultants navigate a muddled analytics landscape and, with your guidance, produce beautiful visualizations from data chaos. Because the entire spectrum of the data process can be daunting, we're here to help with the technical nuances of data warehouse integration to the art of data visualization.

Our clients benefit from our teams of talented consultants, who consistently prove their ability to solve problems and execute solutions. We're excited about the work this publication highlights to showcase our firm's talent. We produced this book in hopes that you'll invite us along your analytics journey. Working together with motivated clients, we seek to help organizations and individuals make better, more informed decisions.

CPSIA information can be obtained at www.ICGtesting.com
Printed in the USA
LVIW01n0117280318
571222LV00002BB/5